THE SCHOOLS HISTORY PROJECT
S·H·P
OFFICIAL TEXT

MAKING SENSE OF **HISTORY**

1066–1509

IAN DAWSON

NEIL BATES

ALEC FISHER

RICHARD MCFAHN

DYNAMIC
LEARNING

HODDER
EDUCATION
AN HACHETTE UK COMPANY

The Schools History Project

Set up in 1972 to bring new life to history for students aged 13–16, the Schools History Project continues to play an innovatory role in secondary history education. From the start, SHP aimed to show how good history has an important contribution to make to the education of a young person. It does this by creating courses and materials which both respect the importance of up-to-date, well-researched history and provide enjoyable learning experiences for students.

Since 1978 the Project has been based at Trinity and All Saints University College Leeds. It continues to support, inspire and challenge teachers through the annual conference, regional courses and website: http://www.schoolshistoryproject.org.uk. The Project is also closely involved with government bodies and awarding bodies in the planning of courses for Key Stage 3, GCSE and A level.

Although every effort has been made to ensure that website addresses are correct at time of going to press, Hodder Education cannot be held responsible for the content of any website mentioned in this book. It is sometimes possible to find a relocated web page by typing in the address of the home page for a website in the URL window of your browser.

Hachette UK's policy is to use papers that are natural, renewable and recyclable products and made from wood grown in sustainable forests. The logging and manufacturing processes are expected to conform to the environmental regulations of the country of origin.

Orders: please contact Bookpoint Ltd, 130 Milton Park, Abingdon, Oxon OX14 4SB. Telephone: +44 (0)1235 827720. Fax: +44 (0)1235 400454. Lines are open 9.00a.m.–5.00p.m., Monday to Saturday, with a 24-hour message answering service. Visit our website at www.hoddereducation.co.uk

© Ian Dawson, Neil Bates, Alec Fisher, Richard McFahn

First published in 2014 by

Hodder Education,

An Hachette UK company

338 Euston Road

London NW1 3BH

Impression number 10 9 8 7 6 5 4 3 2

Year 2018 2017 2016 2015 2014

Cover photo © Image Asset Management Ltd/SuperStock

Artwork by Barking Dog Art, Richard Duszczak, Peter Lubach, Tony Randell and Sebastian Quigley

Design layouts by Lorraine Inglis Design

Typeset in PMN Caecilia Light 10/13pt

Printed in Italy

A catalogue record for this title is available from the British Library

ISBN 978 14718 06681

The Publishers would like to thank the following for permission to reproduce copyright material:

Photo credits

Text acknowledgements

Contents

Investigating the Middle Ages

The people you are going to investigate in this book lived in the Middle Ages, the period of history from 1066 to 1509. The two most important words in the last sentence are PEOPLE and INVESTIGATE.

History is all about PEOPLE – how they lived, what they did, what ideas they had.

You will INVESTIGATE by:

- asking questions about people's lives
- working out what pictures and documents from the Middle Ages tell us about those people
- suggesting answers to your questions.

So let's start straightaway with your first investigation – or enquiry, which is another word for investigation. This enquiry on pages 2–7 explores one of the most famous and astonishing events in the Middle Ages!

A

B

King Henry II made a hasty journey across England. When he reached Canterbury he leaped from his horse and took off his royal clothes. He put on simple clothes and went into Canterbury Cathedral. There he lay down and prayed for a long time.

Then King Henry allowed each of the **bishops** to whip him five times. And after that the monks who were there (and there were a large number) each whipped the king three times.

A monk called Ralph Diceto wrote this description of events in July 1174. Ralph was writing a few years after these events.

← An illustration drawn in the 1200s (the thirteenth century).

Enquiry Step 1: First evidence – asking questions

1 Look carefully at illustration A on page 2. What do you think is happening in this picture?

2 Read extract B on page 2. Explain in a sentence what is happening.

3 Can you think of any way in which the events in A and B might be connected?

4 What questions do you want to ask about these events?

How to carry out your enquiry

Throughout this book you will carry out a number of enquiries. We have called these enquiries 'stepped enquiries' because they take you through a series of steps before you complete them by answering the main question. This page explains what these steps are.

Enquiry Step 1: First evidence – asking questions

You will look at one or two pieces of evidence, such as A and B on page 2. This 'first evidence' has been chosen to take you into the heart of the enquiry, to make you curious and start asking questions about these pieces of evidence. Asking good questions is one of the most important skills in History.

Enquiry Step 2: Suggesting an answer

In Step 2 you will look at more evidence and then suggest a possible answer to the main question you will be investigating. This question is called the 'enquiry question'.

Another word for a possible answer is a hypothesis. So if we ask you to come up with a hypothesis it means: 'Can you suggest a possible answer?'

Enquiry Step 3: Developing your answer

In Step 3 you will look at more evidence and think again about that hypothesis – your first answer. Does this new evidence help you improve your answer or do you have to change it or adapt it?

Enquiry Step 4: Concluding your enquiry

At the end of the enquiry you will use the evidence you have gathered to answer the enquiry question. You will also need to decide how definite your answer is, using words such as 'definitely', 'probably' or 'possibly'.

Why was King Henry being whipped?

In Clue B on page 2 you read about King Henry II being whipped. A king being whipped is so unusual that we have to ask 'Why?'

By the end of page 7 you will have built up a clear answer to that question. Our next step – Step 2 – is to examine some more evidence. Clues C, D and E tell you about King Henry II and another remarkable man, Thomas Becket, and about a truly astonishing event.

Henry II, 1133–89 (reigned 1154–89)

King Henry was a very energetic, intelligent man and a great soldier. He became King of England in 1154 when he was 21. He ruled a huge empire which included much of France as well as England.

Henry was famous for his terrible temper. One writer at the time said that one day Henry got so angry that he could not control himself. He rolled round on the floor and chewed the rushes that were used then instead of a carpet.

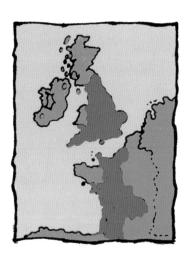

⬆ This map shows Henry II's empire (the areas shaded in red). This empire is called the Angevin Empire because Henry came from Anjou in France and so his family were known as the Angevins.

C

King Henry II in **coronation** robes. ➡

D

King Henry made Thomas Becket the Archbishop of Canterbury in 1162. The Archbishop was the most important churchman in England. Becket had been Henry's friend for many years.

However, King Henry and Becket then quarrelled over who should choose new bishops. King Henry said he should choose the bishops but Becket said that the Pope should choose the bishops. The Pope was the head of the whole Christian Church and lived in Rome in Italy.

Henry was so angry that Becket fled abroad and lived in exile in France from 1164 to 1170 to escape from the quarrel.

E

Becket returned to England in 1170 but the quarrel was not over. What happened next was described by Edward Grim, a monk who saw Becket murdered in Canterbury Cathedral. This is what Edward Grim wrote:

The murderers came in full armour, carrying swords and axes. The monks shouted to the Archbishop to escape but the Archbishop refused.

In a mad fury, the knights called out 'Where is Thomas Becket, traitor to the King and to the country?' The Archbishop, quite unafraid, answered, 'Here I am, no traitor to the King but a priest.'

'You shall die this instant,' they cried. They pulled and dragged him, trying to get him outside the cathedral, but they could not do so. Then a knight leapt at him and wounded him in the head. Another knight struck him on the head but still he stood.

At the third blow he fell to his knees, saying in a low voice, 'For the name of Jesus I am about to die.'

The next blow cut off the top of his head and blood white with brain and the brain red with blood stained the floor.

Enquiry Step 2: Suggesting an answer

You have now looked at five clues A–E. It's time to begin thinking of possible answers to your enquiry question: Why was King Henry being whipped?

Here is a possible answer (hypothesis):

King Henry was whipped because he was sorry that he had quarrelled so badly with Becket, that Becket had to go to live in France.

1 What evidence from clues A–E might support this answer?

2 Do you think this answer is:
   ▌certainly ▌probably ▌possibly ▌definitely not
   the answer?

3 Suggest your own possible answer. Write it out clearly and note down any evidence that supports your answer. You will need this answer when we get to Step 3.

Enquiry Step 3: Developing your answer

Clues F, G and H give you more evidence. Read these new clues and then look again at your answer to question 3 on page 5.

a If you still think it is right, note down any more evidence that supports your answer.

b If you think it may be wrong change it to a new answer and note down the evidence that supports the new answer.

If you do think your first answer was wrong – don't worry!
Historians often change their minds when they find new evidence.
That first answer was only a suggestion so if you now think it was wrong it shows that you're learning!

F

In 1170 Becket returned to England. He was met by cheering crowds. When Henry heard this, he lost his temper and shouted out: 'Are all my men traitors and cowards? Why do you let this low-born priest treat me with such contempt?' Four of his knights set off for Canterbury.

G

As soon as Henry heard that Becket had been murdered, he burst into tears. He spent three days shut in his room, not eating or drinking. He said that he had never meant for Becket to be killed.

H

In 1173, three years after the murder of Becket, there was a great rebellion against King Henry. His own wife and sons allied with the Kings of France and Scotland and fought against Henry. He was in danger of losing many of his lands.

In 1174 Henry asked the Pope for support against his enemies. The Pope said that both he and God would support Henry if Henry showed how sorry he was for Becket's murder. He said Henry must let himself be punished and give land and money to the Church. That was when Henry set out to go to Canterbury to be punished.

Main events 1170–74

December 1170

- Becket returned from exile in France.
- Becket was murdered in Canterbury Cathedral.

1173

- Rebellion against Henry involving his sons and the Kings of France and Scotland.

1174

- The Pope said he would support Henry against rebels if he showed sorrow for Becket's murder.
- In July, Henry II was whipped by bishops and monks at Canterbury.

Enquiry Step 4: Concluding your enquiry

It is time to use the work you have done in Steps 1–3 to answer the enquiry question:

Why was King Henry being whipped?

1 You need to support your answer with evidence. The more precise evidence you use the better.

Use the sentence starters below to help you if needed.

I believe that King Henry was whipped because …

I think this because …

(back up your answer with evidence from pages 2–7)

2 You also need to show how certain you are. Where would you stand on the line of certainty below? Explain why you have made that choice.

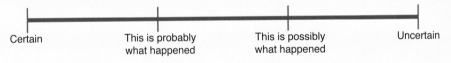

Certain | This is probably what happened | This is possibly what happened | Uncertain

What happened next?

Two days after Henry was whipped, his army captured the King of Scotland. Then he beat the rest of the rebels. Many people said that God gave him the victory because he had shown how sorry he was for Becket's death.

Welcome to the Middle Ages!

The Middle Ages. What a boring name for a period that's full of really interesting history! This was the time when the **Normans** conquered England at the **Battle of Hastings** (but only just!), when the **Black Death** killed nearly half the population, when people lived in simple homes but built sky-scraping cathedrals and when amazing inventions such as printing changed the way we live. It was the time when elephants and a polar bear were kept in **the Tower** of London, when doctors tasted their patients' urine to decide what was wrong with them, and when football was banned by law.

So when *was* the Middle Ages? You can see it on the timeline, divided into two parts. First came the Early Middle Ages (which is also known as **Saxon** and **Viking** England) and then came (surprise!) the Later Middle Ages. It's the Later Middle Ages we'll be investigating in this book. The dividing line between 'Early' and 'Later' was one of the most famous events in British history – the Norman Conquest of 1066.

Activity

Where on the timeline would you find:
- the Norman Conquest
- the Industrial Revolution
- the Tudors
- the Victorians?

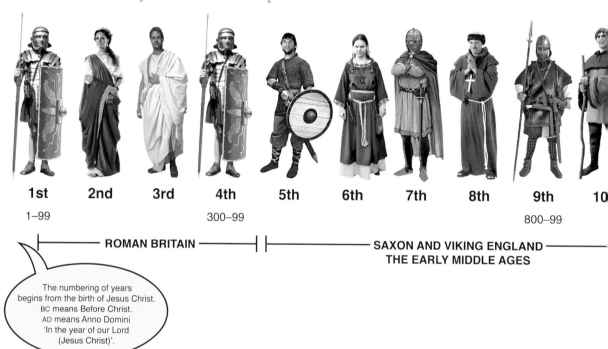

1st	2nd	3rd	4th	5th	6th	7th	8th	9th	10
1–99			300–99					800–99	

├────── ROMAN BRITAIN ──────┤ ├────────── SAXON AND VIKING ENGLAND ──────
THE EARLY MIDDLE AGES

The numbering of years begins from the birth of Jesus Christ. BC means Before Christ. AD means Anno Domini 'In the year of our Lord (Jesus Christ)'.

The Middle Ages – in the middle of what?

The Middle Ages came 'in the middle' between two groups of people. The first group were the Ancient Greeks and Romans. The second group were the people of the Renaissance in the fifteenth and sixteenth centuries. The people who lived during this Renaissance period looked down on the people of the Middle Ages – as you can see in the illustration at the bottom of page 9.

Middle Ages – medieval
The Middle Ages is also called the medieval period. The word 'medieval' comes from two Latin words 'medium aevum' which mean Middle Ages.

Does the timeline show all of British history?

No! People have been living in Britain for many centuries. If we drew a human timeline showing you when the first people lived in Britain we'd have to add another 5000 people to the left-hand end of the line. This is because the first people lived in Britain about 500,000 years ago.

The most famous ancient monument in Britain is Stonehenge, built about 2300BC. How many people would you need to add to the left-hand side of the timeline to go back to Stonehenge?

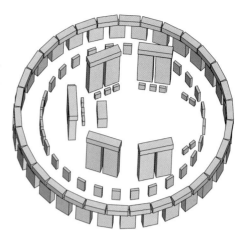

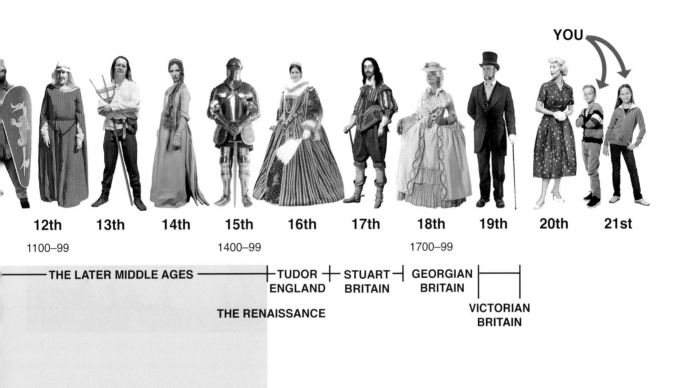

| 12th | 13th | 14th | 15th | 16th | 17th | 18th | 19th | 20th | 21st |

YOU

1100–99   1400–99   1700–99

THE LATER MIDDLE AGES ─────┤ TUDOR ┼ STUART ┤ GEORGIAN ├──┤
                             ENGLAND BRITAIN   BRITAIN

THE RENAISSANCE   VICTORIAN
                                               BRITAIN

Greeks and Romans

The Middle Ages

The people in the middle

We admire the Greeks and Romans for their scientific discoveries, books and wonderful buildings. We will copy and improve their ideas.

We look down on the people in the Middle Ages between us. They didn't do anything important.

Renaissance

Meet the people of the Middle Ages

You are going to meet lots of interesting people in this book, people of all kinds. In the Middle Ages people believed that there were three kinds of people. They were:

- the fighters – the king, his lords and knights
- the people who prayed – the priests, monks and nuns
- the people who worked – the common folk, who were usually farmworkers.

These pages tell you a little more about these three groups of people.

The fighters

The king was the most important man in the country. People believed he was chosen by God to rule England. His main task was to defend his people from invaders and from criminals.

The lords were the king's main supporters and advisers. The king gave them land, often in many parts of the country, so they were very rich. In return they were expected to bring their own soldiers to fight for the king in wartime. They were also expected to keep law and order in their own lands.

> **These are all words that more or less mean the same as 'Lords':**
> - **Barons** ■ **Nobles** ■ **Earls** ■ **Dukes**

⬆ A fourteenth-century drawing of a king hunting with his hawk.

Knights often owned a handful of villages in one area of the country. This meant they were much better off than the common folk and, of course, they did not work. They fought for the king and their lords in wartime. If they did very well in war they might become richer or even be made a lord.

The wealthy wives and daughters of the fighters did not just sit at home and sew while their lords went to war. They were often well-educated and their task was to make sure everything ran smoothly at home while the men were away. They looked after finances, organised the rebuilding and defence of castles and made sure taxes were paid. Many of them did this better than the men!

⬆ A fifteenth-century tapestry showing a lord and lady.

The people who prayed

People believed that this life was a short preparation for a much longer and more important life after death. They believed that Heaven and Hell were real places and so priests were very important because their work and prayers helped people go to Heaven after they died.

There was a priest in every village and everyone was expected to go to church because prayer helped them reach Heaven. There were also many **monasteries** and **convents** around the country where monks and nuns held services of prayer at least eight times a day.

There was only one religion in Britain, Christianity. Other religions such as Islam had not yet reached Britain.

⬆ Monks did a lot to help the poor as well as spending their days in prayer.

The people who worked

Over 90 per cent of people worked as farmers, growing the food to keep everyone well-fed and safe from starvation. For part of each week they worked on the lands of their lord because he would not be digging and sowing crops himself! The rest of the week they worked on their own land.

Some of these people were free but many were **villeins**. Villeins were not free to leave their village or marry without the permission of their lord. They had to work for their lord or face punishment.

Some common folk lived in towns where they worked in all kinds of jobs. Some were **merchants** who became rich selling food or clothes or luxuries. Many others did very ordinary jobs such as raking the streets clean of muck or working as servants.

⬆ Fourteenth-century illustrations showing villagers at work.

Could people become wealthier and move up in the world?

It was very difficult for most people to move up in the world. It required a lot of luck, intelligence or bravery. Sometimes soldiers won land and wealth through bravery in battle. Very intelligent boys could become priests and then rise up to become bishops in the Church. This kind of change became more common later in the Middle Ages (in the 1400s). A good example is the Paston family from Norfolk. In the 1300s the Pastons were ordinary farmers but in the 1400s William Paston became a judge and his grandson, John, was a knight who knew the king. You'll find out in Section 5 why people could move up in the world more easily in the 1400s than before.

Activity

1 What did the lords and knights have to do in return for the lands they were given?
2 What did many wealthy ladies do while their husbands were away at war?
3 Why were priests such important people?
4 What kind of work did most people do?
5 Would you have liked to have been a villein? Explain your answer.

What were the headline events of the Middle Ages?

Eleventh century

1015
- King Canute of Denmark conquered England.
- England stayed part of the Danish empire until 1042.

1066
- At the Battle of Hastings William, Duke of **Normandy**, defeated King Harold of England. Harold was killed and William became King of England.

After 1066
- The Normans ruled England despite English rebellions.
- The Normans built many castles to control the English.
- The Normans also rebuilt many cathedrals and **abbeys**.

1085–87
- The **Domesday Book** – a survey of the value of every village in England – was compiled.

1099
- Christian soldiers from all over Europe took part in the First **Crusade** and captured Jerusalem from its Muslim rulers. Jerusalem is a holy city for both religions.

Twelfth century

1154
- Henry II became king and also ruled much of France. His lands are called the Angevin Empire because Henry came from Anjou in France.

1170
- Thomas Becket, Archbishop of Canterbury, was murdered. Four knights murdered him because they thought King Henry II wanted Becket killed.

1187
- A Muslim army led by the great soldier, Saladin, beat the Christian army at the Battle of Hattin and recaptured Jerusalem. This led to another crusade to recapture Jerusalem.

1192
- Richard I (the Lionheart), King of England, came close to recapturing Jerusalem in the Third Crusade but failed.

Thirteenth century

1204
- King John lost his lands in Normandy. This ended the link between England and Normandy begun in 1066.

1215
- King John faced a rebellion by his barons. John had to agree to **Magna Carta**. This was a set of rules about how the king should govern the country. John soon broke his word and died in the middle of a **civil war** with many of his barons.
- Good harvests led to people being more prosperous. The population grew, perhaps to as many as 6 million people by 1300. New towns were founded and cathedrals were rebuilt and enlarged.

1250s
- King Henry III quarrelled with his barons. They said he was not consulting them about important decisions. Henry was forced to call his barons to meetings three times a year. These meetings were called parliaments.

1280s–1290s
- Edward I conquered Wales, building castles to keep control. He invaded Scotland but did not conquer it.

Fourteenth century

1314

- The Scots army led by Robert Bruce beat Edward II's English army at the Battle of Bannockburn and ended the threat of conquest by England.

1315–19

- A series of very bad harvests led to many deaths from starvation.

1327

- Edward II was the first king to be **deposed** by his nobles .
- Edward II was replaced by his son, Edward III. He was a great soldier who began the **Hundred Years War** against France and won great victories at Crécy (1346) and Poitiers (1356).

1348

- A disease known as the Black Death killed nearly half the population. It was spread by fleas living on rats. Outbreaks continued until the 1370s. The population fell to less than 3 million.

1381

- The Peasants' Revolt was a protest by ordinary people about the failures of the government and heavy taxes. The leaders were killed but people won more freedoms in the long run.

1399

- Richard II was deposed. This was because he would not listen to his nobles. He was replaced by his cousin, Henry IV.
- Sheep farming made many people wealthy. Farmers sold wool for making into clothes and cloth. This was the main industry in England. A great deal of wool and cloth were sold abroad.

Fifteenth century

Throughout

- Living standards improved for many people. They had better houses and food. Many more children learned to read. Merchants selling wool and cloth overseas were very wealthy. They paid for many churches to be rebuilt.

1415

- The **Battle of Agincourt** was a great victory for a small English army over a large French army. Henry V conquered northern France and the English stayed as rulers of Normandy until 1450.

1455

- The Battle of St. Albans was the first battle of the **Wars of the Roses** – a series of disputes between nobles over who would be the best king to make the country strong and peaceful. It lasted on and off for over 30 years. The wars included the Battle of Towton (1461), the largest battle ever fought in England.

1470s

- The invention of printing was brought to England from Europe by William Caxton.

1485

- The Battle of Bosworth was won by Henry Tudor who killed Richard III. This was the beginning of the Tudor dynasty (family of monarchs).

1490s

- The first voyages from England to the Americas.

Activity

We have included these two pages so you can easily check when the most famous events took place. However, History is not just a list of dates and events to be learned – like tables in maths. As you have already discovered, in History you have to think for yourself and suggest answers to questions. The questions below will start you thinking about the most important questions you will be investigating later in this book.

1. What did these kings have in common?
   - John ▌Henry III
   - Edward II ▌Richard II
2. Name two kings who successfully fought battles abroad.
3. What did the barons expect good kings to do? (Use your answers to questions 1 and 2 to help you.)
4. Identify two events that suggest that religion was very important to people.
5. Identify two things that made people's lives very miserable.
6. What evidence can you find to show that people's lives improved at some times?

The Norman Conquest is one of the most famous events in British history. Most people in Britain have heard of the Norman Conquest and the Battle of Hastings. 1066 – the date of the conquest – is one of the most famous dates in all history. Many people visit Norman castles or go to the battlefield every year to watch the battle being re-enacted.

However, famous events are not always significant. To be significant a historical event has to be … well, what do you think?

Here are four events from before that famous date of 1066 that were definitely significant but in different ways.

Activity

1 Work with a partner. Make a short list of reasons why you think a historical event could be significant. Use the events below to help you suggest ideas.

The Neolithic Revolution, c.8000–6000BC

This was the time when people gradually gave up following and hunting herds of animals for food. Instead they began to become farmers, growing their food and settling in one place. This changed the way people lived – forever!

The Roman Conquest of Britain, 43AD

It took 50 years for the Roman legions to conquer most of Britain. Britain became part of the Roman Empire and was ruled by Roman governors. The Roman legions built forts, roads and the first towns which had public baths and fresh water supplies. However, all this disappeared when the legions left Britain around 400AD.

The arrival of the Anglo-Saxons, c.400–600AD

The Anglo-Saxon peoples migrated to Britain from northern Europe. Some were soldiers but many were farmers with their families. These people gave their name to this country – Angle-land became England. Their language also became the language everyone spoke. It is the core of the language we still speak today.

The kings of Wessex unite England, 870–950AD

Until the 900s England was split into several separate kingdoms. Then the Kings of Wessex (Alfred, Edward and Athelstan) united England for the first time. Now everyone had the same king and the same laws. This has continued ever since.

Can you predict the answer to our big question?

By the end of this section (on page 39) you will have built up a good answer to our big question **Was the Norman Conquest really so significant?** However, you don't have to wait until page 39 to start thinking about your answer!

As you saw in Section 1 being good at History is not about waiting to be told the answer to a question. The best historians ask good questions and are good at thinking for themselves by suggesting possible answers to those questions. So let's start thinking now even if you don't know much about the Norman Conquest.

Activity

2 The pictures below show the three groups of people you met on pages 8–9.
   a) Which group do you think the Norman Conquest was most likely to affect?
   b) Which group do you think the Norman Conquest was least likely to affect?
   (If you don't know anything about 1066 or the Norman Conquest think about what a 'conquest' might involve.)
3 Which of these aspects of life in England do you expect were most changed by the Norman Conquest? Explain your choices.
   ▌ The royal family   ▌ Farming   ▌ Language   ▌ Medicine   ▌ Landownership
4 Do you think that the Norman Conquest will turn out to be really significant or just famous? Suggest at least one reason for your answer.
5 What questions do you want to ask about the Norman Conquest to help you with this investigation?

⬆ The fighters – the king, his lords and knights.

⬆ The people who prayed – the priests, monks and nuns.

⬅ The people who worked – the common folk.

How confident was William of Normandy before the Battle of Hastings?

On 5 January 1066 the king of England died. King Edward the Confessor had been a peaceful man who never fought a battle. In contrast, his successor, King Harold, had to fight two battles to keep his crown. He won the first but lost the second to William, Duke of Normandy.

However, William's victory was far from certain. William had faced major problems before his army even landed in England. Harold was a good, experienced soldier. So how confident was William as he waited for battle? That's your enquiry on these two pages.

William was born around 1027, the son of the Duke of Normandy. William's father died when he was just seven. By the time he was fifteen he was fighting to keep his **Dukedom** against rival lords. He quickly learned his skills as a soldier and how to be ruthless in war.

During the 1030s a young English lord called Edward arrived in Normandy. Edward should have been king of England but Danish kings had conquered England and taken the crown. William allowed Edward to live in exile in Normandy until he was able to return to England in 1042 and become king. Edward was very grateful to young Duke William for helping him. As a result, Edward promised in 1051 that William would be his successor as king.

William's hopes of the crown grew stronger in 1064 when Harold Godwinson, Earl of Wessex, arrived in Normandy. Harold was the most powerful lord in England. According to the story William told later, Harold promised to help William become the next king of England. One version of this story is shown in a scene in the **Bayeux Tapestry** below.

 A

Duke William of Normandy.

Harold with his hands touching two boxes. The crosses on the box on the left suggest it contained something of religious importance, perhaps the bones of a **saint**.

This scene in the Bayeux Tapestry shows Harold taking an oath while he was in Normandy. The Tapestry was planned and designed by the Normans although it was woven in England within a few years of 1066. The writing in this scene does not say what oath Harold took, but Norman chronicles say that Harold's oath was a promise to help William become the next king of England.

1066 – the invasion of England

Despite King Edward's promise William did not become king when Edward died. Instead Harold took the crown, chosen by the **Saxon** lords. William said that Harold had broken his oath and recruited an army to invade England. He built ships which he stocked with weapons and food. Finally, just before the ships were ready to sail, the **cavalry** horses were taken on board.

But all that summer William's invasion was delayed by the wind blowing strongly against his ships and stopping them sailing. Would William's men abandon the invasion? Was the delay giving Harold the chance to strengthen his defences?

In late September 1066 the wind changed and William set sail. The Normans did not know what to expect. Would there be a Saxon army waiting to throw them back into the sea? William knew that Harold was a successful and experienced soldier. He did not know that King Harold had marched north to fight the **Viking** army.

With no Saxon army to stop them, the Normans landed safely but did not move far from the coast for fear of being cut off from their ships. The Bayeux Tapestry shows them looting, stealing food, setting fire to local houses and building a castle.

It was 13 October when William's scouts brought news that Harold and his army were approaching. William ordered his men to spend the night wearing their armour, weapons close at hand. Now 38 years old and a very experienced soldier, he knew that the next day he would be fighting for the crown of England.

Activity

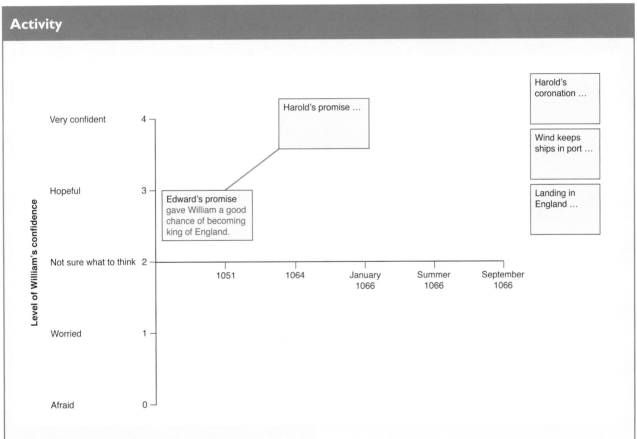

1 Draw a copy of this graph. Complete the sentence beginning 'Harold's promise' to show why William's confidence increased in 1064.
2 The three boxes alongside the graph need to be added to it. Take each one in turn and add it to your graph using these instructions:
   a) Decide William's level of confidence. Add the box at the right level on the graph.
   b) Complete the sentence in each box to explain why William felt more or less confident.
   c) Continue the line between the boxes showing the rise and fall of William's confidence.
3 William must have felt anxious, but also confident that he could beat Harold. Why do you think he was confident of winning?

Why did William win the Battle of Hastings?

A

⬆ A modern reconstruction of the end of the **Battle of Hastings**.

Enquiry Step 1: First evidence – asking questions

Look at illustration A above.
What questions does it make you want to ask about the battle?

It was the evening of 14 October 1066. The fighting had begun early in the morning and was now finally over. The Normans had achieved a hard fought victory and the victims of the slaughter lay all around. Amidst the horror, King Harold's mistress, Edith Swan-Neck, finally identified his body.

Meanwhile, William Duke of Normandy, vowed to thank God for granting his victory by building a fine church on the spot where Harold had planted his **standard**. William held true to his promise and you can visit Battle Abbey today. But what were the more earthly reasons for William's victory that day?

⬆ Battle Abbey, Hastings, today.

Before the battle

In the summer of 1066 King Harold expected that Duke William would invade. But as the summer wore on, the Normans did not arrive as the wind held them back from sailing (see page 17). Harold had to disband his army because his men needed to go home to collect the harvest. Not long after that, events suddenly changed, as you can see from map B.

B

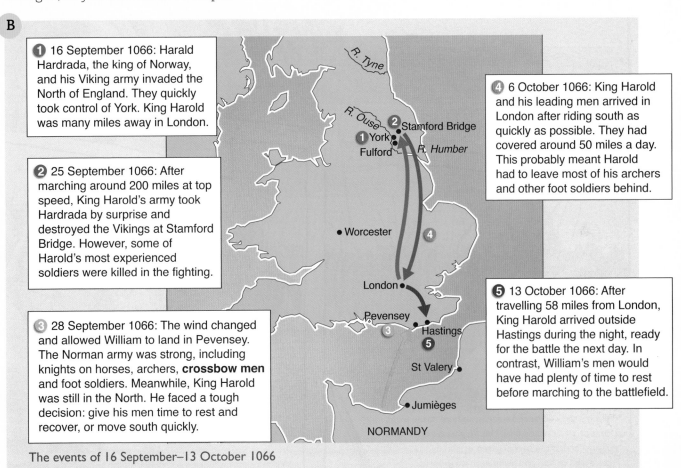

1 16 September 1066: Harald Hardrada, the king of Norway, and his Viking army invaded the North of England. They quickly took control of York. King Harold was many miles away in London.

2 25 September 1066: After marching around 200 miles at top speed, King Harold's army took Hardrada by surprise and destroyed the Vikings at Stamford Bridge. However, some of Harold's most experienced soldiers were killed in the fighting.

3 28 September 1066: The wind changed and allowed William to land in Pevensey. The Norman army was strong, including knights on horses, archers, **crossbow men** and foot soldiers. Meanwhile, King Harold was still in the North. He faced a tough decision: give his men time to rest and recover, or move south quickly.

4 6 October 1066: King Harold and his leading men arrived in London after riding south as quickly as possible. They had covered around 50 miles a day. This probably meant Harold had to leave most of his archers and other foot soldiers behind.

5 13 October 1066: After travelling 58 miles from London, King Harold arrived outside Hastings during the night, ready for the battle the next day. In contrast, William's men would have had plenty of time to rest before marching to the battlefield.

The events of 16 September–13 October 1066

Enquiry Step 2: Suggesting an answer

Now it's time to identify some of the reasons that helped William to win the Battle of Hastings.

1   Use map B above to copy and complete the cards below. You are making cards so that you can group your ideas and support your thinking later. The first one is done for you.

> Some of Harold's men were exhausted after marching north, defeating the Vikings and travelling back south as quickly as possible.

> William had made excellent preparations. His army was made up of …

> Harold lacked some of his most experienced men at Hastings because …

2   Find more reasons that might have helped William win the battle. Make a card for each one. Remember to write in full sentences.

3   Which of your reasons so far do you think was the most important in helping William to win? Why?

The Battle of Hastings

The Battle of Hastings began around 9a.m., 14 October 1066. Some historians say William had kept his men ready throughout the night in order to prevent a surprise attack. King Harold's army had taken position at the top of the hill. The English lacked archers, which meant they could not attack the Normans from distance.

Here, on foot, they drew close together and formed a shield wall to protect them from Norman arrows and attacks.

William's army advanced steadily, archers at the front, then foot soldiers and finally his knights on horseback. William carried the banner given to him by the Pope, a sign to him and his men that God was on their side.

William sent his knights to try and smash through the shield wall. However, riding uphill soon tired the horses and the Normans failed to make a breakthrough. The fighting continued for another couple of hours, both sides hacking away at each other as the Normans made continued attacks on the shield wall.

After a few hours a rumour went round that William was dead. Some Normans began to flee. Just at that moment William appeared and rushed towards them shouting, 'Look at me! I am alive and with God's help I will conquer!' Bravely he led his men in another attack.

William encouraged his men to use the trick of retreating. They pretended to run away and some of Harold's less experienced soldiers left the shield wall to chase them.

Away from the safety of the shield wall, these men were quickly surrounded and hacked to death by the Norman knights on horseback.

Slowly the shield wall began to grow weaker, as Norman arrows and further attacks began to wear Harold's army down. Finally, as dusk fell, King Harold was killed. Without their leader, Harold's army began to flee. The battle was over and William was victorious.

Enquiry Step 3: Developing your answer

The storyboard on pages 20–21 outlines the events of the Battle of Hastings. Read it to find as many reasons as you can that helped William to win.

1 Copy and complete the two examples below.

> William's men must have felt confident that God was on their side because …

> William showed he was a good leader when …

2 Make cards for the other reasons you found in the storyboard. Remember to write in full sentences.

3 Now look at the reasons collected so far in Enquiry Steps 2 and 3. Which do you think was the most important in helping William to win? Why?

Enquiry Step 4: Concluding your enquiry

Over the last few pages you have discovered a lot of reasons why William won the Battle of Hastings. You produced cards in Enquiry Steps 2 and 3 to show these. Now you are going to sort these cards in different ways to help you think about how they link together and which were the most important.

Making links

Historians need to be good at seeing how reasons for events can link together.

1 Go through your cards and find one reason that led to or caused another. Find as many pairs as you can. Make sure you can explain how one reason led to another. An example is given below.

> The wind changed just at the right time for William, while Harold was still in the North.

This meant that …

> Some of Harold's men were exhausted after marching north, defeating the Vikings and travelling back south as quickly as possible.

Organising the causes

Historians also like to understand the reasons for events by putting them into groups.

2 Put your cards under the following big headings (group of reasons):

Harold's weaknesses and bad luck

The strength and skill of the Norman army

William's leadership

3 Now it is time to decide on your answer to our enquiry question. Which of the three big headings above do you think was the most important reason why William won the battle? Explain why you chose it. Use your answers to questions 1 and 2 above to help you. Discuss this with a partner or as a class.

Communicating your answer

Now you can use the work you have done in Enquiry Steps 1–4 to write an essay in answer to the enquiry question:

Why did William win the Battle of Hastings?

Your essay should contain the following things:
■ Introduction – this is where you outline the question and grab the attention of the reader.
■ Paragraphs – this is the main part of the essay where you examine the reasons William won.
■ Conclusion – this is where you give a judgement about which reason was most important.

Writing an introduction

An introduction should grab the attention of the reader and briefly outline what the question is about. Have a look at this one we have written for you:

> In 1066 two armies met. The battle lasted most of the day. King Harold of England was killed and the winner became the new king of England. We need to look at the reasons why William was able to win.

1 Rewrite our introduction in order to improve it. Think about the following before you rewrite it:
■ What factual details could you add to it?
■ Does it grab the attention of the reader?
■ What words and phrases could you use to make this better? Below are some ideas.

> ■ bloody ■ violent ■ dramatic ■ Duke William of Normandy ■ brave ■ Hastings ■ Harold's weaknesses and luck ■ William's leadership ■ the strengths and skills of the Norman army ■ 14 October 1066

Writing paragraphs

A good essay is structured into paragraphs. Your three big headings will each become a paragraph in your essay. A good paragraph is like a good burger, both have key ingredients (see page 23). Without a top bun (opening point), there is nothing to hold the meal together. If you miss out or don't add enough meat (evidence) the burger is tasteless. If you forget the bottom bun (the explanation) the meat (evidence) falls out and is useless!

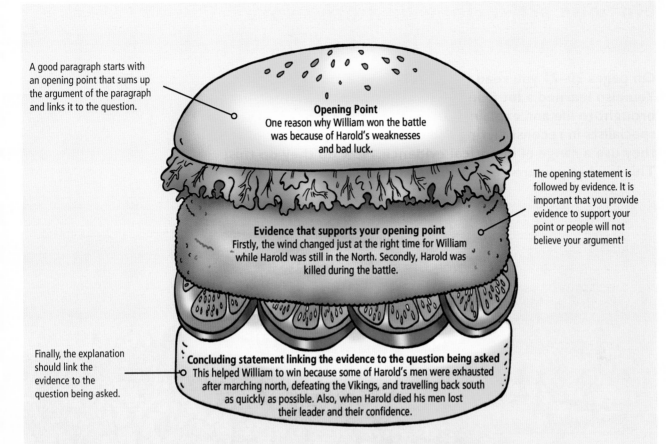

A good paragraph starts with an opening point that sums up the argument of the paragraph and links it to the question.

Opening Point
One reason why William won the battle was because of Harold's weaknesses and bad luck.

The opening statement is followed by evidence. It is important that you provide evidence to support your point or people will not believe your argument!

Evidence that supports your opening point
Firstly, the wind changed just at the right time for William while Harold was still in the North. Secondly, Harold was killed during the battle.

Finally, the explanation should link the evidence to the question being asked.

Concluding statement linking the evidence to the question being asked
This helped William to win because some of Harold's men were exhausted after marching north, defeating the Vikings, and travelling back south as quickly as possible. Also, when Harold died his men lost their leader and their confidence.

2 Write your own paragraph about the evidence for your next big heading. Remember to use the key ingredients. Use the sentence starters below to help you if needed.

Point	Evidence	Explanation
A second reason William won the battle was the strength and skill of the Norman army. A final reason William won was …	For example … Firstly … Moreover … Furthermore … Secondly … Lastly … Finally …	Therefore, William was able to win because … This meant … This led to … This resulted in …

3 Now that you are feeling confident, write the next paragraph on your own. Remember to start with an opening point, back it up with evidence and then explain how this links to the question. The table above will give you some prompts if you need them to start your sentences.

Writing a conclusion

Your conclusion should let the reader know which reason you think was the most important in helping William to win the battle. You already thought about this in Enquiry Step 4. The sentence starters below will help you:

Overall, I think the most important reason William won the Battle of Hastings was …

This is because …

Has our artist done his homework? Reconstructing the Battle of Hastings

On pages 20–21 you read the story of the Battle of Hastings. You also learned a lot from the illustrations. History is often brought to life and explained through pictures. Some artists are specialists in reconstructing the events of the past. To do this they use a range of historical evidence. How do they do this? This is what you are going to investigate.

A ⬇ A reconstruction of the Battle of Hastings by the artist Peter Dunn.

This reconstruction of the Battle of Hastings (picture A) is by the artist Peter Dunn. It was painted well over 900 years after the battle. There is no direct archaeological evidence from the battle site, so how did Peter Dunn know it looked like this?

Activity

I Can you find the following features in picture A?

1 Norman knights on horseback

2 Some English soldiers with facial hair, unlike the Normans

3 Norman arrows flying towards the English and sticking in their shields

4 The Saxon shield wall

5 King Harold's red dragon of Wessex banner

6 More English soldiers arriving to fight on foot

7 A Norman with a sword sticking in his chest

8 An English housecarl wielding a double-handed battleaxe

9 Both sides wearing chainmail and using swords

10 Facial expressions of fear, tiredness and anger

Evidence from chroniclers

Often artists get the idea of what to draw *directly* from the evidence. For example, the account from the Norman Chronicle in extract B mentions Norman knights on horseback. So, Peter knew to include this in his picture. Sometimes evidence might not say or show something directly but the artist looks for clues, reads between the lines and makes an **inference**. For example, extract B says that the Normans had archers, so we can infer some English shields would have had arrows sticking in them. Extracts B, C and D are from some of the chroniclers Peter Dunn read whilst working on his reconstruction.

B

William's troops advanced in good order, the men armed with bows and crossbows were at the front. Then came the infantry and at the rear were the cavalry.

Harold's large army came from every part of the country and was reinforced by the Anglo-Saxon's allies, the Danes. They took to the higher ground, a hill close to the forest through which they had come. They went on foot and drew themselves up close one to the other.

The sound of trumpets announced the start of the battle. The Norman infantry attacked but were driven back by spears, stones and other English missiles. Then the cavalry rode into battle using their swords. Both sides fought fiercely. The English were helped by the higher position they held and remained tightly grouped.

A Norman account by William of Poitiers, written around 1071. He was not at the battle.

C

William had arrived with a countless number of horsemen, slingers, archers and foot soldiers. Harold immediately marched to London even though he knew many of his bravest soldiers had already fallen in the battles in the North.

An English account by John of Worcester, written around 1071. He was not at the battle.

D

Coming on grouped together, the English seized possession of the hill and stood fast on foot. On the highest point of the summit the king planted his banner and other standards.

A Norman account by Guy, Bishop of Amiens, written around 1068. He was not at the battle.

Activity

2 Copy and complete the table below listing features 1–10 from Activity 1 on page 24. The first two have been done for you.
   a) Which features in picture A are *directly* mentioned in extracts B, C and D?
   b) Which features in picture A might have been *inferred* from extracts B, C and D? Explain why.
   A feature might come directly from one source *and* be inferred by others. Some of the features might not be not directly mentioned or inferred in extracts B, C and D – so you may have gaps in your table.

Features	Comes directly from	Inferred from (with reasons)
1 Norman knights on horseback	B, C	
2 Some English soldiers with facial hair, unlike the Normans		

Evidence from the Bayeux Tapestry

Peter Dunn made extensive use of the Bayeux Tapestry during his research. The tapestry was woven in England a few years after 1066. It was planned and designed by the Normans. The original is around 70 metres long! Below and on page 28 are some scenes from the tapestry.

E

↑ Norman soldiers on horseback.

F

↑ Norman archers.

G

↑ Norman knights charge the English shield wall.

⬆ English soldiers with battleaxes.

⬆ English and Norman soldiers fighting.

⬆ An English soldier holds the red dragon banner for all to see.

⬆ English soldier struck down by a Norman knight.

Activity

3 Add to your table from Activity 2 on page 26. This time look at how the evidence in E–L (pages 27–9) might have been used to create picture A on pages 24–5.

a) Which features in picture A are *directly* shown in E–L?

b) Which features in picture A might have been *inferred* from E–L? Explain why. Remember, a feature might come directly from one source *and* be inferred by others.

Evidence from the battlefield today

As part of preparing to create his picture, Peter visited the site of the battle and did a careful survey. This helped him to picture the landscape on which the fighting took place and the position of the two armies.

↑ The battlefield today. The abbey shows where the English lined up to fight.

> The other aspect of producing these reconstructions was emotional rather than academic. The accounts of the fighting made my blood run cold: the noise, English shouts of Oli crosse, Godemite and ut, ut, screams of men and horses, sweat, fear.

↑ The artist Peter Dunn.

Activity

4 Which of the statements below do you think best sums up how Peter Dunn created picture A on pages 24–5? Give reasons for your decision.
   a) Peter Dunn only used details taken *directly* from the evidence to create picture A.
   b) Peter Dunn relied mainly on *inferences* he made from the evidence to create picture A.
   c) Peter Dunn used an *equal mix* of details he *inferred* from the evidence and details taken *directly* from the evidence to create picture A.
   d) A statement of your own!
5 Read what Peter says on the left about creating his reconstruction of the battle. Was he right to use his imagination and emotions? Or should he have relied only on the historical evidence? Give reasons.

What kind of king did William become?

William was now King of England – but would the English build up another army and rebel against him? Could he control the whole of England when he had only 7000 men? There were over 2 million English people! William was also still Duke of Normandy and his enemies in France might attack Normandy while he was in England. These dangers in both England and Normandy influenced what kind of king William turned out to be. On pages 30–31 you will find out whether he treated the English generously or harshly.

William's thoughts in 1066

Here is what William thought in 1066 after the Battle of Hastings.

I want to stay King of England and Duke of Normandy. I need to be free of rebellions and attacks in both countries.

I will let most English lords keep their lands so they have no reason to rebel against me. I will give my Norman friends the lands of the English who died fighting against me in battle.

I will treat the English fairly so that they do not rebel against me. If they rebel I will have to spend time fighting in England. This will give my enemies in France the chance to attack Normandy.

William's thoughts in the 1080s

I have had to treat the English harshly because …

When I am in England there is always danger in …

I have taken the land of nearly all the English lords because …

When I am in Normandy …

Activity

1 However, things did not work out the way that William hoped. By the 1080s his thoughts must have been very different. Read page 31 and draw your own version of the diagram on the left, completing William's thoughts in the 1080s.

2 Choose TWO words that you think best describe how William ruled England.

Rebellions in England

Despite his victory at Hastings, William was anxious about English rebellions. He was right to be worried. From 1067 to 1071 there were rebellions all around the country. The most dangerous was in the North in 1069. Rebels killed the Norman commanders in York and Durham, while a Danish army invaded the North and helped the rebels. William must have feared he would lose his crown. He marched north rapidly and frightened off the Danes. Then he made sure there would be no repeat rebellion by destroying homes and crops and killing people and farm animals across the North. This 'Harrying of the North' was a terrible act of cruelty.

After the rebellions had been crushed, William took nearly all the land away from English lords and gave it to his Norman supporters. This meant that English leaders had far less power and wealth.

Dangers in Normandy

William's other great worry was whether he could keep control of his homeland of Normandy, especially at first when he had to stay in England most of the time because of the rebellions. This gave his enemies in France the chance to attack Normandy. In 1079 William even had to fight off a rebellion led by his own son, Robert! These threats to Normandy meant that after 1072, William spent 80 per cent of his time in Normandy. When William died, he was still fighting in Normandy, as he had done all his life.

Trouble in England

In the 1080s William's absence in Normandy meant more trouble in England. The Scots attacked northern England. In 1085 a Danish fleet threatened another invasion. That threat led William to order the Domesday Survey. **Domesday Book** recorded who owned every village and what each village was worth. William probably wanted to make sure he could raise enough taxes and men in case he had to fight off another invasion.

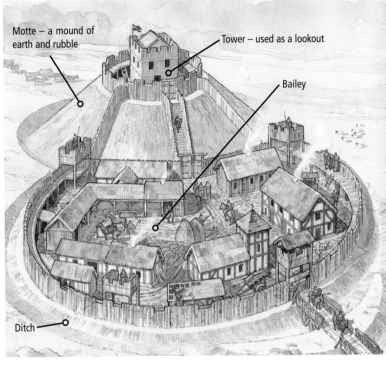

Motte – a mound of earth and rubble

Tower – used as a lookout

Bailey

Ditch

⬆ The Normans built many simple motte and bailey castles. At first they were built of wood. This meant they could be built quickly but still provide Norman soldiers with defences in case they were attacked by the English.

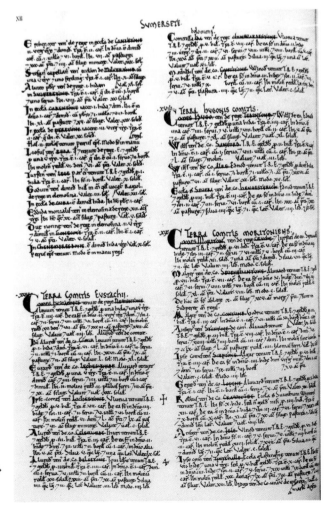

This page from Domesday Book lists some of the land in ➡ Somerset owned by three Normans, Earl Eustace, Earl Hugh and the Earl of Mortain.

Stepped Enquiry

Was 1066 a disaster for everyone?

In 1087 King William was still fighting. He had just captured a French town when his horse was frightened by a burning flame. The horse reared up. William was violently thrust onto the iron pommel on his saddle, splitting his stomach open. He was taken to a **monastery** to be nursed but the wound was fatal. As he lay dying his once loyal supporters raced off to secure their land and property. His servants stole his jewels and clothes, leaving his rotting body naked. The man who had spent his life taking whatever he could, was, at the end, robbed of everything – even his dignity.

After William's death the monk who wrote the *Anglo-Saxon Chronicle* gave his verdict on William's life, shown in extract A on the right.

A

King William was greater and stronger than all the kings before him. He was kind to the good monks who served God. During his reign, the great Cathedral of Canterbury was built and so were many others. He was cruel to anyone who disobeyed him, putting lords and even his own brother in prison. He kept good order in the country. A man with a bag of gold could travel unharmed right through the country. No man dared kill another.

The king raised castles and crushed the poor
He took gold and silver and so much more
There was no fairness in his deeds
He simply fed his deepest greed
He loved to hunt for stags and boars
He took our land and made this law
The eyes of poachers who steal from their Lord
Must be cut out with the point of a sword.

Enquiry Step 1: First evidence – asking questions

Read extract A from the *Anglo-Saxon Chronicle*.

1 List two things that William had done that the monk thought were successful.

2 List two things that William had done that the monk thought were cruel.

3 What questions do you want to ask to help you decide if 1066 was a disaster for everyone in England?

Enquiry Step 2: Suggesting an answer

You already know a lot about the Norman Conquest so we can go straight to suggesting an answer to our enquiry question:

Was 1066 a disaster for everyone?

1 Below you can see a 'Disaster–Success' line. Draw your own copy. Where on the line do you think the following people would go? If they probably thought the Norman Conquest was a disaster put them somewhere near the 'Disaster' end. If they probably thought it had been a great success then put them somewhere near the 'Success' end.
a A Norman lord who had fought alongside William at Hastings.
b A Saxon lord who survived the Battle of Hastings.
c A Saxon peasant living in Norman England.
d A Saxon monk who wrote the *Anglo-Saxon Chronicle*.

2 Look at the pattern of people on the line. Sum up your answer to the enquiry question in a sentence.

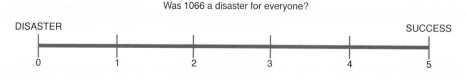

Was 1066 a disaster for everyone?

DISASTER   SUCCESS

0   1   2   3   4   5

Saxon lord: Thorkell of Arden

Look at the scars on my arms. Can you see the wounds that I got at the blood bath they now call the Battle of Hastings? I saw nearly all my friends die on that battlefield. I was loyal to good King Harold, and fought alongside him. But when he died I had to make some important decisions. You see, I own large areas of land in Mercia. I love the power it gives me, and I love acting as a judge.

But it wasn't always like this. After Hastings, I feared for my life and my lands. William took all the lands of one of my good friends Cuthbert and left him with nothing – no land and no loyal men. Cuthbert was imprisoned. I thought that the same thing would happen to me. I lived in fear that I would lose everything. That is why I decided to swear loyalty to the new king, William. He has been generous to me. He let me keep my land as long as I work for him. I think he knew that I was a good soldier and have many loyal, well-equipped men who are always willing to fight for me. He can now call on them.

By backing William I managed to keep my land and my title. But I lost the respect of some of my Saxon men. They thought I was a traitor. However, the money and power make up for it. I am still very wealthy. But my life has changed in many ways – every time I attend the king's court everyone speaks in French! I have had to learn this difficult language very quickly.

The law has become much harsher. William expects judges like me to punish law breakers ruthlessly. More and more criminals are hanged. More laws are written down, in Latin.

I sometimes mix with William's Norman men. They have strange short haircuts and are much more religious than the old Saxon lords. It is hard to understand what they say. Many things have changed for me since Hastings. But I have to keep looking to the future and thank God for what I still have.

Enquiry Step 3A: Developing your answer

1 Place Lord Thorkell where you think he should go on the Disaster–Success line from Enquiry Step 2.
2 Explain why you have chosen this place for Thorkell.
3 Write a speech bubble above Lord Thorkell on the line to sum up his opinion of the Norman Conquest.

Norman lord: Alan of Richmond

Come in, come in – welcome to my new castle. It has only just been finished. It helps me control the large areas of land which I now own. I am known as Alan of Richmond here in England. But back home I am Alan of Brittany. I came over with William in October 1066. I fought alongside him at the Battle of Hastings. What a terrifying battle. Every night I give thanks to God for our victory.

My loyalty to the king has served me well. I own vast amounts of land here in England, right across the country, further than the eye can see. My loyal men look after this land for me. They control large areas for me. They also own hundreds of thousands of Saxon peasants who farm the land for us.

William has always valued my opinions. Even before we took over this green country I advised the Duke. I still do. I have more wealth, and I'm more important than I have ever been. I still speak in French, with the other Normans who came over to rule here. Many of my friends are now great barons – we meet up sometimes at the king's court and swap stories of our times back in France. I sometimes miss my friends at home – I own land in Brittany too, but don't get back as much as I'd like. There is too much to do here you see.

Enquiry Step 3B: Developing your answer

1 Place Lord Alan where you think he should go on the Disaster–Success line from Enquiry Step 2 (page 32).

2 Explain why you have chosen this place for Alan.

3 Write a speech bubble above Lord Alan on the line to sum up his opinion of the Norman Conquest.

Saxon peasant: Edith, from Bovey, Devon

Welcome to our humble home. My husband built it with his hands, using the knowledge that was passed down to him by his father.

We are simple farmers. Our families have farmed these strips of land ever since God made the Earth. Our forefathers have ploughed the fields and sowed the seeds in exactly the same way that we do. If the harvest is good we are happy because our stomachs are full.

We are blessed with two fine sons: Alfred and Stephen. Yes, I know Stephen is an unusual name. These new foreign names are all the rage at the moment.

Stephen was very ill last year. He nearly died. Luckily my mother is an expert in medicine. Her grandmother taught her how some wild plants have magical healing qualities. We pass on our knowledge. She used these cures to nurse our son back to health.

What's that? The Normans – how have they treated us? How dare you mention them in my house! Earlier this year Norman men came intruding into our lives, requiring answers to questions about the way we lived and what we owned. Why do they want to know such things? Why can't they leave us in peace? They wanted to know exactly how much land we owned, how many sheep, how many oxen and how many cows we have. They then wrote all of this information down and took it away. We still live in fear that they will come back and steal the little that we have to survive on. The Normans are a dreadful people.

Enquiry Step 3C: Developing your answer

1 Place Edith where you think she should go on the Disaster–Success line from Enquiry Step 2 (page 32).
2 Explain why you have chosen this place for Edith.
3 Write a speech bubble above Edith on the line to sum up her opinion of the Norman Conquest.

Saxon monk: Brother Eadwine, from Glastonbury Abbey

Be quiet, talk in a whisper! My brothers and I should spend most of our waking hours in silence.

I thank the Lord for my life, but I struggle to thank the Lord for the Norman invasion. I am a humble monk and I have devoted my life to God. Each day I pray, study religious books, farm the land and sleep. Before the Normans came we were happy in our mission and did our work in our own Saxon way. Sometimes we didn't follow *all* the rules as they were intended, but we loved our Saxon **abbot**, who led us and turned a blind eye to our sins. We worked hard and generally lived a good life.

But soon after the Normans invaded, things changed dramatically. Nearly every Saxon abbot across the country has been replaced by a Norman. Nearly all the archbishops are now Norman too. What happened to the good Saxon abbots and archbishops, you ask? Many of them have been locked up. Their crime? They are simply *suspected* of hating the Normans.

Between you and me, many of us do quietly hate the Normans. They have changed the way we live. They have tried to make our lives stricter and even more religious. Also, William now requires each **abbey** to provide money to pay for his army. This means that instead of focusing on God's work, we have to spend our time trying to make money. We now sell the vegetables we grow in order to pay the king. We previously used this food to feed the poor.

Many of my brother monks have refused to obey our new Norman Church leaders. We know that the Normans are deeply religious men and want to improve our religious ways, but we loathe the changes. Here at Glastonbury our hated new Norman abbot, Thurston, changed the way we chanted our prayers. This was the final straw. How dare he! When we refused, he acted without mercy. He sent in a group of Norman knights to attack us. They shot arrows at us and used swords and knives to murder three of our brothers. Eighteen more were wounded. At least King William acted in our favour. He sent Thurston back to Normandy in disgrace. I just hope that God can forgive him, and William, for all that they have done to ruin our lives.

Enquiry Step 3D: Developing your answer

1 Place Brother Eadwine where you think he should go on the Disaster–Success line from Enquiry Step 2 (page 32).

2 Explain why you have chosen this place for Brother Eadwine.

3 Write a speech bubble above Brother Eadwine on the line to sum up his opinion of the Norman Conquest.

Saxon peasant: Brom, from Haxby, Yorkshire

Welcome! I'd offer you some food but I barely have enough to feed myself. You must have travelled up through York? Did you see all of those rotting corpses? The whole place is a shadow of its former self. When the Normans first arrived, little changed, life went on as normal. But then, last year, in 1069 the people of the North felt powerful enough to stand up to the Normans. Backed by invaders from Denmark, they started a rebellion. They attacked the Norman soldiers at the new castle they had built. The people of the North took control.

Everything seemed fine. But then thousands of the Norman troops arrived. They burnt down every house in our village – broke our tools, murdered our children and set all of our crops on fire. They attacked every village in this area. Over 600 houses in York were destroyed. Thousands have died. We have no harvest. My wife and two of my children starved to death. The only way I have survived is through poaching. I hunt at night and catch all kinds of animals on the land that the Normans stole from us. This is a terrible risk because of William's new harsh laws. If I am ever caught, I could be blinded or, worse still, executed.

Enquiry Step 3E: Developing your answer

1 Place Brom where you think he should go on the Disaster–Success line from Enquiry Step 2 (page 32).

2 Explain why you have chosen this place for Brom.

3 Write a speech bubble above Brom on the line to sum up his opinion of the Norman Conquest.

Enquiry Step 4: Concluding your enquiry

When you look at your completed Disaster–Success line you can see that some people benefited from the Norman Conquest but others did badly. This tells us two important things about people in the past: that people's lives were different even if they lived in the same period of history, and even if they lived in the same country.

It is time to use the work you have done in Steps 1–3 to answer the enquiry question:

Was 1066 a disaster for everyone?

In your answer you need to consider:

- What kinds of people benefited? Why?
- What kinds of people suffered? Why?
- The numbers of people who suffered compared with the numbers of people who benefited.

You might want to use the sentence starters below to help you get started:

1066 was a disaster for some people. For example …

Other people's lives improved after the Norman Conquest. For example …

Overall the Norman Conquest was … This was because …

The Big Picture

Was the Norman Conquest really so significant?

Now that you know the dramatic story of 1066 and you have investigated the events of William the Conqueror's reign it's time to return to the question we introduced on pages 14–15 and decide whether the Norman Conquest was really significant as well as being famous.

You have already found out how the Normans affected the lives of people at the time, people such as Thorkell, Alan, Brom, Brother Eadwine and Edith whom you met on pages 33–37. Their lives did change, sometimes a great deal. You will need to use that information in the activity below. However, first you are going to investigate a new question:

Did the Norman Conquest continue to affect life in Britain for centuries afterwards?

1 Death and destruction

Many English people died in battle and in rebellions against the Normans. Homes, crops and animals were destroyed by the Normans to punish rebels. Homes were also destroyed to make space for castles.

Activity

1 Draw your own version of the 'ripple diagram' below. Then decide where on the diagram each card on pages 38–39 should go. There is one example on the diagram to show you how to fill it in.

2 Look at the pattern of cards on your completed diagram. Use it to write a short answer to the question:

Did the Norman Conquest continue to affect life in Britain for centuries afterwards?

3 Now think back over all your work on the Norman Conquest. In your opinion, was it a significant event in British history? To answer this question:
   a) Think about how the Conquest affected people at the time and people over future centuries.
   b) Explain whether you think it was significant or not.
   c) Choose three pieces of evidence to support your answer. These should provide evidence of the impact of the Norman Conquest both at the time and over later centuries.

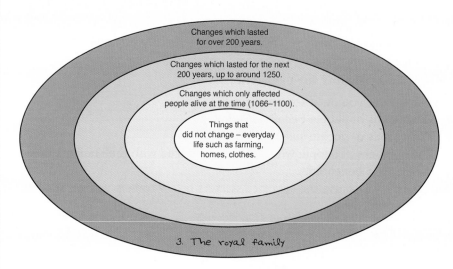

2 Castles

The Normans built castles all over England to control the English. These castles were rebuilt many times and continued to be used as homes for centuries. Some still survive.

5 The ruling class and landowners

The Saxon lords who advised the king and held most of the land in England were replaced by William's Norman supporters. By 1087 England had a completely new ruling class of landowners. Some of these families continued to own these lands and play a leading part in government for hundreds of years after 1066.

8 Religion, cathedrals and monasteries

William and his lords were deeply religious and determined to make England a more religious country. They rebuilt over half the cathedrals. These became much larger with the latest fashions in architecture from France. New monasteries were built too and, by the 1130s (70 years after the Conquest), there were four times as many monasteries, monks and nuns. These new cathedrals and monasteries were still being used in the 1500s. Some cathedrals are still in use today.

3 The royal family

A new dynasty (royal family) became kings of England from 1066, replacing the Saxon kings. The distant descendants of the Norman kings still reign in Britain today.

6 Language and names

portcullis archer

Robert

The language spoken in England changed after 1066. French words used by the new ruling class gradually became part of the English language, although English words remained in the majority. Examples of French words which became English are archer, baron, sausage, roast, tax, moat, duke, portcullis. Some French names such as William, Robert, Richard and Alice also became popular.

9 The power of the king

William the Conqueror was the most powerful king England had ever had. He said that he owned all the land in the country and could give land (or take it away) from even his strongest barons. Kings remained extremely powerful until the seventeenth century when they first began to share power with Parliament.

4 Links with Normandy

Before 1066 England had close links with Scandinavia (Denmark, Norway and Sweden) but in 1066 England became part of the Anglo-Norman empire. Kings of England were often away in Normandy and other parts of France, fighting to defend their French lands. This continued until 1204 when King John lost Normandy to the King of France.

7 One country, two peoples

1066   1200

After 1066, the English did not feel they were living in their own country any longer. They were frightened of Norman soldiers on horseback, wearing chainmail and speaking a language they couldn't understand. Who knew if they were talking about dinner or killing all the local villagers? The new lords saw themselves as Normans, not English, so England was a country of two different nationalities. However, this changed gradually in the 1100s, partly through marriages between the English and Normans. By 1200 the divisions between Normans and English had mostly died out.

Stepped Enquiry

3

Why did people in the Middle Ages build glorious cathedrals but live in such simple houses?

Why did people in the Middle Ages build glorious cathedrals but live in such simple houses?

Welcome to Durham Cathedral, one of the first cathedrals to be rebuilt by the Normans after the Conquest. Even today, when we are used to skyscraper buildings towering over cities, Durham Cathedral is awe-inspiring. Walk around it. Even better, walk into it and the power and majesty of the building is stunning.

Building Durham Cathedral today would be a huge task, even with modern technology and skilled workers used to immense engineering projects. But building this cathedral over 900 years ago was even more remarkable. This enquiry and this whole section explore why people built such glorious cathedrals and what that tells us about the people of the Middle Ages.

A ⬇ Durham Cathedral.

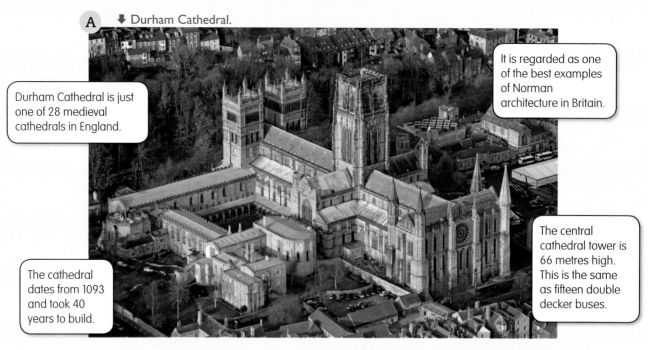

Durham Cathedral is just one of 28 medieval cathedrals in England.

It is regarded as one of the best examples of Norman architecture in Britain.

The cathedral dates from 1093 and took 40 years to build.

The central cathedral tower is 66 metres high. This is the same as fifteen double decker buses.

B

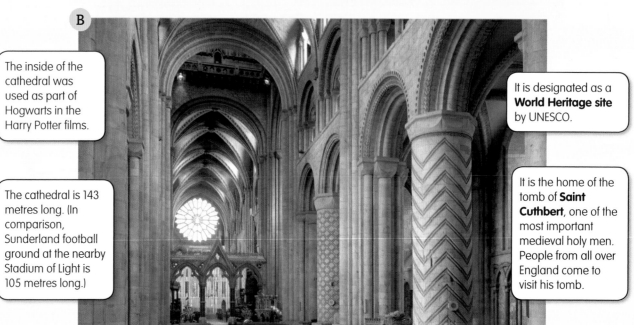

The inside of the cathedral was used as part of Hogwarts in the Harry Potter films.

It is designated as a **World Heritage site** by UNESCO.

The cathedral is 143 metres long. (In comparison, Sunderland football ground at the nearby Stadium of Light is 105 metres long.)

It is the home of the tomb of **Saint Cuthbert**, one of the most important medieval holy men. People from all over England come to visit his tomb.

In the picture below you can see a medieval peasant's house.

C

In some villages houses were divided into two sections: one for sleeping and the other for keeping animals safe at night.

The roofs were thatched. There was little furniture and straw was used for lining the floor.

Houses such as this were often rebuilt, perhaps every 30 or 40 years.

Windows were holes in the walls covered by wooden shutters as glass was very expensive.

Most ordinary people lived in a house like this when Durham Cathedral was being built in the eleventh and twelfth centuries.

Peasants' houses were built around a wooden frame onto which was plastered wattle and daub. This was a mixture of mud, straw and manure. The mixture would dry in the sun and form a strong building material.

Enquiry Step 1: First evidence – asking questions

1 Look at the pictures in A, B and C. What similarities and differences can you find between the two buildings?

2 What questions do you have about these buildings or the people who built them?

Enquiry Step 2: Suggesting an answer

In picture D you can see Conall, the son of one of the authors of this book when he visited Durham Cathedral. After the visit Conall wanted to know why people in the Middle Ages built glorious cathedrals but lived in such simple houses. What answers can you suggest to Conall's question?

D

⬆ Conall standing in front of Durham Cathedral.

3

Why did people in the Middle Ages build glorious cathedrals but live in such simple houses?

Stepped Enquiry

Conall decided to use an internet search engine in order to find an answer to his question. He received the reply shown in E below.

E

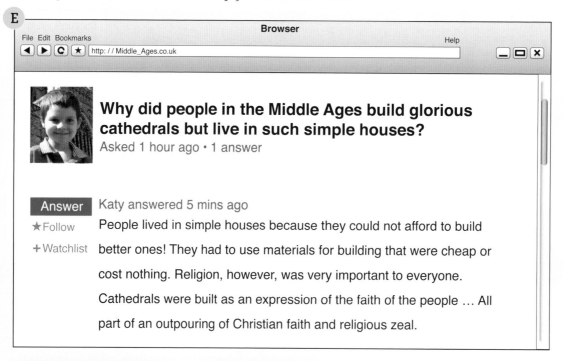

Browser

File Edit Bookmarks   Help

◀ ▶ C ★ http:// Middle_Ages.co.uk

Why did people in the Middle Ages build glorious cathedrals but live in such simple houses?

Asked 1 hour ago • 1 answer

Answer   Katy answered 5 mins ago

★ Follow   People lived in simple houses because they could not afford to build

✦ Watchlist   better ones! They had to use materials for building that were cheap or

cost nothing. Religion, however, was very important to everyone.

Cathedrals were built as an expression of the faith of the people … All

part of an outpouring of Christian faith and religious zeal.

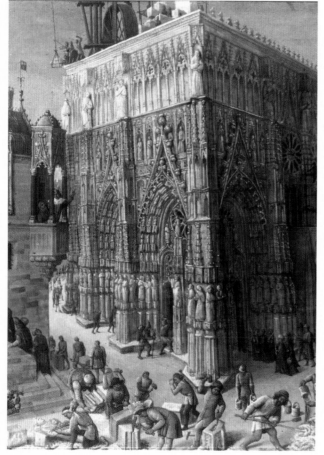

⬆ This picture of cathedral building in the 1400s shows how much work and human effort is needed. The energy, time and money spent on building show how important cathedrals were.

Think

Read the answer to Conall's question in E above. Do you think it is right about why people had such simple houses? Can you sum up in a couple of words the reason it gives why medieval people built such glorious cathedrals?

Enquiry Step 3: Developing your answer

The internet answer provides a good explanation of why people built simple houses but is the internet answer about why they built such glorious cathedrals good enough? Your task is to decide whether it was simply religious belief that explains why people built such huge cathedrals. Look at picture F on page 43. It shows a master **mason** thinking about the reasons why he has been asked to build a cathedral. The master mason was the man in charge of the whole building project. He played a big part in designing the cathedral. He also chose the workers to employ and the stone and other materials that were used.

1 Read the thought bubbles. Which of them suggest religious reasons for building a cathedral?

2 What other types of reasons can you see? Try and come up with two more categories.

F

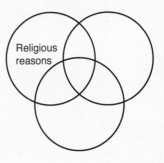

1 People have a strong belief in God. Building a cathedral will be a sign of their faith.

2 Myself and the other masons will make the city proud by building a great cathedral to rival all others in its size and splendour.

3 Pilgrims will visit the cathedral, bringing money for the Church and businesses in the town.

4 The Church will give **indulgences** (a pardon for our sins) for people who helped to build a church or cathedral. These will help us all get into Heaven.

8 The tall spires and large stained glass windows will encourage people to reach towards heaven and bring people closer to God.

7 A cathedral will remind people who is in charge. By helping to pay for a cathedral, the king is showing off his wealth and power.

6 This cathedral will be a clear sign of the wealth and the power of the Church.

5 Building this cathedral will give us a great sense of achievement. We will have been part of something special and we will have played our part in bringing glory to God.

Enquiry Step 4: Concluding your enquiry

It is time to use the work you have done in Enquiry Steps 1–3 to answer the enquiry question:

Why did people in the Middle Ages build glorious cathedrals?

As historians we need to organise the information we have collected in order to answer a question. One way to organise our information is to use a Venn diagram like the one on the right.

1 Make a copy of the Venn diagram in your notebook. We have labelled one circle but labelling the other two is your task. Use your answer to question 2 in Enquiry Step 3 on page 42 to label the other two circles.

2 Read through the thought bubbles in picture F again. Now add the numbers or a brief description of each point into the correct circles of your Venn diagram.

3 What does your completed Venn diagram tell you? Talk with your partner about the following questions:
   a Was it only religious belief that led to people building magnificent cathedrals?
   b Which category had the most reasons?

4 You are now ready to give Conall a better explanation of why people built such glorious cathedrals.
   In your reply you might like to think about the following points:
   a How important was religion in explaining why cathedrals were built?
   b What other reasons were there?
   c How important do you think these other reasons were?

   Also, try to give examples from what you learned from the medieval master mason about why people wanted to build cathedrals.

Religious reasons

3

Why did people in the Middle Ages build glorious cathedrals but live in such simple houses?

Why were Heaven and Hell so important to people?

The great cathedrals tell us that religion was very important to people in the Middle Ages. Pages 44–45 dig deeper into people's ideas to discover some more ways in which religion affected people's everyday lives.

If you had been born in the Middle Ages, you would have seen a picture like the one shown in picture A below every week of your life, on the wall of your local church. This picture is in a church in Surrey in the South of England. Let's take a look at the detail – if you dare!

A ⬇ A medieval wall painting from a church in Chaldon, Surrey showing Heaven and Hell.

Two huge devils boiling murderers in a pot over a fire.

Go to **www.paintedchurch.org/chaldon.htm** to learn more about the painting.

Activity

1 Can you find the following scenes in the picture?
- ▮ The ladder out of Hell with **souls** trying and failing to climb out?
- ▮ A man (representing the **sin of greed**) counting his money while being held in a fire by two devils with fork?
- ▮ The spiked bridge with dishonest tradesmen trying to complete hopeless tasks (such as a blacksmith trying to make a horseshoe without an anvil)?
2 What do you think is happening in scenes A and B?
3 Why do you think pictures like this were painted on church walls?

How could you spend less time in Purgatory?

People believed that their life after death was far more important than their life on Earth. Life on Earth was just a brief preparation for life after death. They also believed that Heaven, Hell and Purgatory were real places. They expected, for example, to walk around these places so people who had had injuries to their legs were sometimes buried with crutches to help them walk.

Only a few people – the **saints** – would go straight to Heaven. Nearly everyone else would spend some time in Purgatory where they would pay for their sins and wait for them to be forgiven. How long anyone spent in Purgatory depended on how sinful they had been and how much good they had done. However, there were ways to reduce the time spent suffering in Purgatory.

B

5 Help improve the lives of people in your town by helping to pay for fresh water supplies or to have streets paved.

1 Leave money to have prayers said for your soul. The richer you are the more prayers you can pay for.

6 If you are wealthy, build a special chapel and employ priests to say prayers for your soul. If you are very wealthy you can have thousands of prayers said each day.

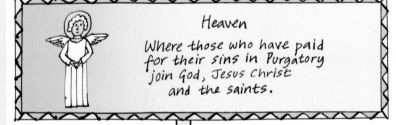

Heaven
Where those who have paid for their sins in Purgatory join God, Jesus Christ and the saints.

Purgatory
Where nearly everyone goes to be punished for their sins. The pains and torments are almost as bad as those in Hell but when people have paid for their sins they go to Heaven.

Hell
Where those whose sins are so terrible they cannot be forgiven go. The pains of Hell are far worse than any pain suffered on Earth.

2 Give money, food, clothes and housing to the poor or leave money in your will to pay for this.

7 Pay for part of your local church to be rebuilt.

3 Go to church every week and pray for forgiveness.

8 Go on **crusade** to win back Jerusalem for Christianity.

4 Pray for the souls of the poor on All Souls Day. This is in November when the poor who could not afford to pay have prayers said especially for them.

9 Go on a **pilgrimage** to Canterbury or Rome or Jerusalem (see pages 46–47). The further you go the more sins will be forgiven.

Activity

The boxes around picture B show a variety of ways to reduce your time in Purgatory.

1. Which methods could only be chosen by the rich?
2. When did the poor get help through Purgatory?
3. What could everybody do to reduce their time in Purgatory?
4. Which were the most dangerous ways of reducing time in Purgatory?

3

Why did people in the Middle Ages build glorious cathedrals but live in such simple houses?

The pilgrimage game

Do you remember the story of Thomas Becket at the beginning of the book (pages 2–7)? The site of Becket's murder was one of the most important places of pilgrimage in the Middle Ages. Thousands of people travelled to Canterbury to pray and so pay for their sins. Some adventurous pilgrims travelled to Rome where the Pope lived, or to Jerusalem where Jesus Christ had been crucified.

Now you can go on a pilgrimage in this board game. On the way you will discover all kinds of ways in which religion affected everybody's daily lives. You will travel from the tomb of Saint Cuthbert in Durham Cathedral to the port of Dover where you can board your ship to Jerusalem.

Activity

Work in groups of 3 or 4. The winner will be the first player to arrive at Dover. Each group will need a dice and counters. Take it in turns to roll the dice and follow the instructions in the square you land on. If it is a picture square just wait until your next go.

1 Use your experiences from the game to draw a spider diagram summing up what you have learned.
   a) In the centre of your spider diagram write 'How did religion affect people's everyday lives?'
   b) Now add to the diagram anything that you learned from the squares that you landed on.
2 Compare your diagram with the one your partner created.
   a) How similar are the two diagrams?
   b) Is there anything that you need to add to your diagram after seeing your partner's?
3 Finally, read the squares that you did not land on. What else can you add to your diagram?

The Big Picture

3

Why did people in the Middle Ages build glorious cathedrals but live in such simple houses?

Religion in Britain before 1500

Cathedrals show how important religion was to people in the Middle Ages but religion had always been important as you can see on these Big Picture pages.

Other gods, other cathedrals

We do not know anything definite about religion before the Roman Conquest. People probably worshipped gods linked to the harvest, seasons and the sun because they depended on warmth, light and food to keep them alive. They had their own 'cathedrals' such as Stonehenge where people probably met at important times of the year.

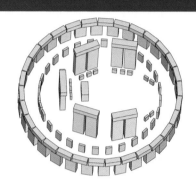

The first Christians

Christianity came to Britain in the Roman period, but we do not know how common Christianity was then. The number of Christians fell when the Roman legions left Britain around AD400. In AD597 the Pope sent monks to convert the Anglo-Saxons in England to Christianity. These monks were led by Augustine. Gradually Christianity spread throughout the country.

Christianity in the Middle Ages

Cathedrals are just one clue about the importance of religion. There were also 900 **monasteries** and over 20,000 monks and nuns. Monasteries employed over 40,000 people as servants, farmworkers, cooks and in other jobs. Priests, monks and nuns looked after the poor and the sick and provided education for clever children. Everyone celebrated holy days because they were holidays.

The Church was very powerful. It owned a lot of land and became very wealthy from farming, especially selling wool from its sheep. Archbishops and **bishops** were very powerful men, often acting as advisers to kings.

Above all religion and prayer were vital to everyone because they helped make sure people did not go to Hell in their next life.

Activity

1 By 1500 had Christianity been the main religion in Britain for
   a) over 5000 years b) just over 900 years?
2 Why were monasteries so important for the people of medieval England?
3 Why was Jerusalem at the centre of Christian maps in the Middle Ages?

The English church – part of a bigger world

⬇ As you can see from this medieval map, Jerusalem was the centre of the Christian world. This map was made in 1275.

Jerusalem is a holy city for Christians. In the city is the Church of the Holy Sepulchre where it is believed Jesus' body was buried before he ascended to Heaven.

In theory the Pope appointed all archbishops and bishops but he usually left the choices to the king.

For Jews, Jerusalem is the site of the Holy Temple, the centre of Jewish worship for centuries.

Pilgrims travelled to Jerusalem from all over Europe. The wars known in Europe as the Crusades (see page 97) were fought over control of Jerusalem.

The English Church was part of a much bigger religious organisation, the Roman Catholic Church. The head of this Church was the Pope who lived in Rome. The Roman Catholic Church was incredibly wealthy, funded by taxes paid by people across Europe.

Jerusalem is also a holy city for Muslims because it was from here that it is believed the Prophet Muhammad was taken up into Heaven.

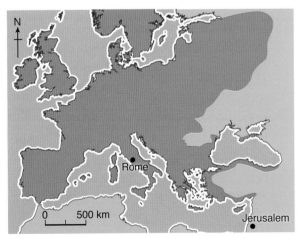

⬆ This map shows the area where Christianity was the main religion. This area was called Christendom.

Activity

It's time to sum up what you have learned in this section. We can do this by looking ahead to the 1530s. That was when King Henry VIII created one of the biggest revolutions in English history by making changes to the country's religion. So here's your last question. Answer this by thinking back over this section.

4 Can you think of three reasons why people in the 1530s might be frightened and horrified by changes to religion?

The Big Picture

As you discovered in section 2, William the Conqueror was an extremely powerful king. To be effective, medieval kings had to win wars, defend England, make the country peaceful and avoid rebellions by keeping the barons happy. These pages allow you to have a quick look to see how effective medieval kings were between 1066 and 1509.

Activity

1 Quick quiz:
  a) Which king died with a red hot poker (apparently)?
  b) Which kings died of old age?
  c) Which kings died of diarrhoea with serious fever? What name is given to this disease?

2 You are going to test three hypotheses (a hypothesis is a theory or an idea). Are they right or wrong? You need to find supporting evidence from the table on pages 50–51 to prove them correct or incorrect. If they are incorrect can you change the wording of the hypothesis to make it correct?

  ▌ All medieval kings were interested in leading their armies well and winning wars with other countries.
  ▌ Most medieval monarchs were very good at keeping nobles happy and avoiding conflict in England.
  ▌ All medieval kings got on with their families.

3 Can you come up with your own hypothesis and test it?

Name and reign	Known for	In England	Abroad	Died
William I (the Conqueror) 1066–87	Conquering England and building castles.	Won the **Battle of Hastings** and crushed rebels.	Won wars and land in France.	Aged 59 after rupturing his stomach.
William II (William Rufus) 1087–1100	Having red hair!	Won the support of barons, avoiding rebellion.	Fought successfully against Wales, France and Scotland.	Aged 40 shot by an arrow while hunting.
Henry I 1100–35	Keeping his eldest brother Robert in prison for life.	Ruthlessly kept England peaceful.	Won **Normandy** from his brother Robert.	Aged 67 of serious indigestion.
Stephen 1135–54	Waging a long **civil war** against his cousin Matilda.	Fought a long civil war.	Did nothing – too busy fighting the civil war.	Aged 58 of a heart attack.
Henry II 1154–89	The murder of Thomas Becket.	Brought the barons under control.	Ruled the huge Angevin empire (covering most of France).	Aged 56 in bed.
Richard I (The Lionheart) 1189–99	Being a great crusader.	Spent only 9 months in England; rebellions broke out in his absence.	Fought in the **Crusades**, nearly captured Jerusalem.	Aged 42, shot by an arrow attacking a town in France.
King John (Lackland) 1199–1216	Being called Lackland or Softsword.	Quarrels with barons and high taxes led to civil war.	Lost all lands in France.	Aged 49 of dysentery (diarrhoea with serious fever).

Name and reign	Known for	In England	Abroad	Died
Henry III 1216–72	Becoming king aged only 9.	Quarrelled with barons led by Simon De Montfort and lost the civil war.	Did very little.	Aged 65, of old age.
Edward I (Longshanks) 1272–1307	Being a great soldier and made his baby son Prince of Wales.	Kept barons happy by involving them in key decisions.	Went on crusade and conquered Wales.	Aged 68 of old age, marching to fight the Scots.
Edward II (1307–27)	Being a weak king and dying a painful death.	Did not listen to his barons which caused civil wars.	Lost to the Scots at the Battle of Bannockburn.	Aged 43. Perhaps murdered with a red hot poker!
Edward III 1327– 77	Being a very successful king.	United his barons by consulting them about his plans.	Won famous battles aganst the French and the Scots.	Aged 65, of old age.
Richard II 1377–99	Ending the Peasants Revolt in 1381 aged 14.	Distrusted his barons causing rebellions.	Made peace with France.	Aged 32, murdered on the orders of his cousin Henry.
Henry IV 1399–1413	Being the first king to speak English as his first language since 1066.	Faced rebellions in England after seizing the crown.	Fought against Welsh rebels.	Aged 47, collapsed in Westminster Abbey.
Henry V 1413–22	Winning the **Battle of Agincourt** in 1415.	Enforced laws and united barons in war.	Won a dramatic victory at Agincourt and conquered half of France.	Aged 35, died of dysentery.
Henry VI: 1422–61, 1470–71	Becoming king aged 9 months old.	Unable to take decisions, leading to civil wars.	Lost English lands in France.	Aged 50, murdered in **the Tower** on Edward IV's orders.
Edward IV 1461–1470, 1471–1483	Being handsome and a great soldier.	Won battles in the **Wars of the Roses** to take the crown.	Invaded France but took a French bribe and left.	Aged 40 after catching an illness perhaps while out fishing.
Edward V 1483	Being one of the Princes in the Tower and disappearing.	No time to rule.	No time to fight.	Aged 12. Was he murdered by his uncle, Richard III?
Richard III 1483–85	Having scoliosis – a twisted spine.	Taking the throne from his nephews caused rebellions.	Frightened the French and Scots so they helped his opponents.	Aged 32, killed at the Battle of Bosworth fighting bravely.
Henry VII 1485–1509	Being the first Tudor king.	Faced rebellions because he did not trust his nobles to support him.	Invaded France but took money to return home again.	Aged 52 after a long illness.

Key

☐ Norman kings   ☐ Angevins   ☐ Plantagenets   ☐ Lancaster   ☐ York   ☐ Tudor

What makes a good medieval king? Case study: Edward III

Edward's father, Edward II, was a very weak king. There were civil wars and lots of crime and chaos in England. He was murdered in 1327 by his wife, Queen Isabella, and her lover, Roger Mortimer. They made 14-year-old Edward, king, but ruled the country for him. Then, when Edward was 18 he had Mortimer arrested and executed and he started to rule England himself.

Now I am king

Edward was tall, strong and an excellent soldier. He knew that the best way to stop quarrels between the nobles was to get them fighting on the same side – in wars against Scotland and France. In 1333 Edward won a great victory against the Scots at the Battle of Halidon Hill.

Next, Edward went to war with France. In 1346, he invaded France and faced a large French army at the battle of Crécy. Again Edward was the winner, thanks to the English knights and archers. The king's 16-year-old son, also called Edward, fought in the heaviest fighting at Crécy. The prince became known as the Black Prince, probably because he wore black armour. Two months later King Edward captured the King of Scotland in the battle of Neville's Cross in the North of England.

Edward was very popular with his nobles. They joined his army because he was successful and because they won land and money. Edward trusted his nobles and asked their advice. His father had been a failure because he did not trust his nobles and because he lost wars with Scotland and France.

Edward always looked and behaved like a king. He loved expensive clothes and jewels. He rebuilt Windsor Castle in an impressive style. He also tried to be like the fictional King Arthur. He held tournaments and jousts where the knights competed for prizes. He called his bravest knights the Knights of the Garter. They were meant to be like King Arthur's Knights of the Round Table.

In 1348 the Black Death reached England. Nearly half the population died from this terrible disease. When it ended, ordinary people thought they could get higher wages because there weren't enough workers, but Edward made a law saying that everyone had to work for the same wages as before the Black Death. This was hard on ordinary people but good for the nobles and other landowners who didn't have to pay out more wages.

The Black Death didn't stop Edward fighting for long, although one of his daughters died of the disease. In 1356 he invaded France again, won the Battle of Poitiers and captured the King of France. He freed the French king in return for a huge ransom and the promise that England could keep a large part of southern France.

You are guilty and will be heavily punished

England was more peaceful while Edward was king. He could not stop all crimes but the worst gangs of criminals were punished. There were no civil wars or rebellions because Edward got on well with the nobles. Edward was also good at getting parliament to give him money for his wars.

Edward's last years were not so successful. As he grew old he became sick. Edward's wife Queen Philippa and many of his old friends died. His new advisers seemed more interested in getting rich than helping the king. Edward was too old to lead his army himself, and France fought back successfully in the war, even raiding the English coast. England lost nearly all its possessions in France.

It was important for a king to have a son. The son automatically became heir to the throne and this meant there were no quarrels about who the next king should be. Edward had many children. His eldest son, the Black Prince, died in 1376, making the Black Prince's son, Richard, heir to the throne. When Edward died in 1377, Richard II became king when he was only 10 years old. Everyone was anxious about whether there would be problems with a child king, but they remembered Edward III as a hero.

Activity

As you discovered on pages 50–51, Edward III is seen as a very successful king. Some historians say he was the greatest king in the Middle Ages. Why was Edward III such a good king? And just how successful was he?

1 Read the story of Edward III on pages 52–53. Make a list of the reasons why he was a good king.
2 Which of these reasons do you think was the most important in helping him be an effective ruler? Why?

Why was Edward III a successful king?

The story on pages 52–53 suggests that Edward III was a successful king. You have already listed some reasons why of your own. In History we need to support our reasons, or points, with evidence. If you look at the portrait of Edward III below you can see the six big points that made medieval monarchs successful.

A king needed to look wealthy and powerful.

A king's main job was to defend his people by leading his army well in wars.

A king needed the support of his most powerful barons.

A king needed to avoid rebellions by keeping the nobles and landowners happy.

A king needed to keep his country peaceful and make his people feel safe.

A king needed a son and heir to rule after him.

⬆ Edward III (king from 1327–77).

Activity

1 Read back over the story of Edward III on pages 52–53 and find as much evidence as you can to support the points about what makes a successful king in picture A. A table has been started below. Copy and complete your own version.

Big point	Supporting evidence
A king needed to look wealthy and powerful.	Edward loved expensive clothes and jewels. Edward rebuilt Windsor Castle in an impressive style.

2 You are now going to write a paragraph explaining why Edward III was a successful monarch. Do you remember the guidance on how to write a good paragraph on page 23? Here it is again:

A good paragraph starts with an opening point that sums up the argument of the paragraph and links it to the question.

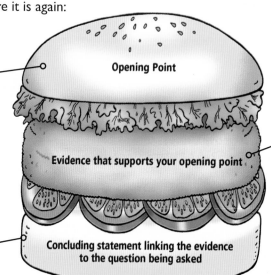

Opening Point

Evidence that supports your opening point

Concluding statement linking the evidence to the question being asked

The opening statement is followed by evidence. It is important that you provide evidence to support your point or people will not believe your argument!

Finally, this should link the evidence to the question being asked.

3 Choose whichever of the following options best suits you.

Option 1 – check our paragraph

Here is a paragraph that someone else has written. Check it against the hamburger guidance. On your own copy underline in different colours:
▌ the opening statement   ▌ the supporting evidence
▌ the concluding statement.

> Edward III was a successful monarch because he looked the part and showed off his power well. For example, he loved expensive clothes and jewels. Furthermore, he rebuilt Windsor Castle in an impressive style which helped people believe he was rich and strong and could protect them. All of this proves that Edward was successful at showing off his power.

Option 2 – use these ingredients to write your own paragraph

Here are the ingredients you need to write a paragraph which answers the question, 'why was Edward III a successful king?' Use it to construct your own hamburger paragraph.

a Choose one of the sentences below as the opening point for the top of your hamburger bun.

b Choose two more sentence starters below to complete as your evidence.

c Now decide what goes into the bottom bun for the concluding statement. You could choose one of our sentences below, or you could write your own – it is up to you.

d Re-read your paragraph. Do you want to make any changes?

> For example, he was successful in battles against the French such as the Battle of …

> Edward III was a successful king because he gained the support of his most powerful barons.

> The evidence suggests that nobles supported him because …

> He also gained the nobles' support after the Black Death because …

> All of this proves that Edward's success was partly down to the fact that he gained the support from his most powerful barons.

Option 3 – do it yourself

If you don't need any help, choose one of the big points from your table to write a paragraph which explains why Edward was a successful king. Use the hamburger approach.

Why did the barons rebel against King John?

Edward III was one of the most successful kings. John was one of the worst, possibly *the* worst king in the Middle Ages. He even managed to lose the crown jewels when his baggage train was caught by the incoming tide as he tried to cross the area of water called The Wash! John's reign (from 1199 to 1216) ended in civil war with some of his barons fighting against him.

So what had John done that was so bad his barons rebelled against him? Let's begin with a picture of John, drawn by the monk and historian, Matthew Paris, in the 1250s. It shows John's crown almost sliding off his head, a sign that there was a lot of opposition to him while he was king.

The picture contains two more clues to John's failure. Can you work out what they are telling us?

Enquiry Step 1: First evidence – asking questions

1 What do you think Matthew Paris, the artist, is telling us about King John in picture A?

2 What questions do you want to ask about John and his reign?

A

Matthew Paris drew pictures of other kings. In all of them the king is shown holding a church up high, to show his support for the Church. Here King John is shown blocking out a church behind him.

Other kings are shown sitting on proper thrones. King John is sitting on a temporary folding stool, the kind used by kings who spent a lot of time travelling to fight wars.

4

Could medieval kings always do whatever they wanted?

'Softsword' – King John's wars

John did spend much of his reign fighting very unsuccessful wars. The maps B and C show you how much land he lost to the king of France.

↑ King John out hunting. John was aged 48 in 1215 at the height of his quarrel with the barons. By then he was fat and bald and he loved fine clothes, especially robes made of fur.

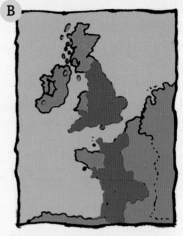

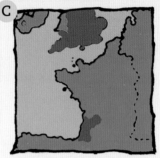

↑ Maps showing the land (in red) John inherited when John became king in 1199 and his land by the end of his reign in 1216.

One of John's difficulties was that King Philip of France was a tough opponent. Philip was determined to take control of English lands in France. These lands had been successfully defended by Henry II and Richard the Lionheart, John's father and brother. Both men had been great soldiers, but once Richard died Philip saw his chance.

Philip skilfully stirred up trouble among John's French barons but John also made mistakes. He made his French barons angry through two bad decisions.

- Firstly, in 1200 John married a rich French girl called Isabella. However, she was already promised to a French baron who complained to King Philip. Philip used the marriage as a perfect excuse to seize John's lands in France.
- Secondly, John had his nephew, Arthur, killed in 1202. Some of John's French barons had wanted Arthur as their ruler instead of John. Rumours spread that John had murdered Arthur in a drunken rage. This angered some of the French barons who now wanted Philip, not John, as their king.

Therefore, John lost supporters in his French lands and was not strong enough to fight Philip. By 1204 John had lost nearly all of his land in France and was given a new nickname, 'Softsword'.

Enquiry Step 2: Suggesting an answer

You now know a little about King John so you can begin to build up your answer to the enquiry question:

Why did the barons rebel against King John?

1 What mistakes did John make as king? It might help to look back to page 54 to see what made Edward III a success.

2 Suggest your own <u>possible</u> answer to the question. Write it out clearly and note down any evidence that supports your answer. You will need this answer when you get to Enquiry Step 3.

Enquiry Step 3: Developing your answer

You probably included John's defeats in war in your hypothesis – your possible answer to the enquiry question from Enquiry Step 2. Now it's time to dig deeper and build up your answer in more detail.

1 These cards show five reasons why the barons rebelled. Make your own set of these cards. Some detail has already been added to the first one.

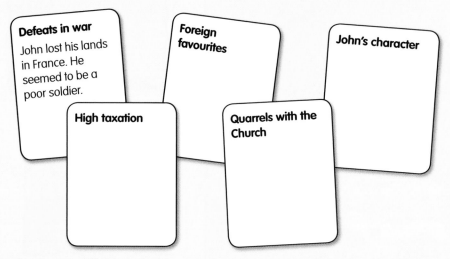

Defeats in war
John lost his lands in France. He seemed to be a poor soldier.

Foreign favourites

John's character

High taxation

Quarrels with the Church

2 Read pages 57–59 and add a sentence or two to each card to show how each reason led to rebellion.

3 Now look again at your answer to the enquiry question from Enquiry Step 2.
   a If you still think it is right, note down any more evidence that supports your answer.
   b If you think it needs improving or changing then write out your new answer, noting down the evidence that supports it.

The quarrel with the Pope

King Philip was not the only opponent King John had to face. The new Pope, Innocent III, was determined to increase the power of the Church throughout Europe. In 1205, Innocent tried to choose the Archbishop of Canterbury even though English kings usually chose their own bishops. When King John disagreed the Pope ordered an **interdict**. This meant that priests stopped all church services. No marriages or burials could take place on Church land.

In 1208 John retaliated by confiscating Church land and property. This raised a lot of money but made his argument with the Pope even worse. In 1209, the Pope **excommunicated** John. This meant John would go to Hell when he died.

Advisers and taxes

John was not good at winning the support and trust of his barons. He often took important decisions without consulting them. They did not see why they should give John money or risk their lives for him when he failed to ask for their advice or listen to them. John preferred the advice of foreign **mercenaries**. He even gave them castles taken from his English barons.

The barons also distrusted John because he kept demanding higher and higher taxes. Barons expected to pay taxes when they inherited their father's land, but they expected to pay the same amount of tax as in the past. John made them pay huge amounts of money, far more than the land was worth. He also made widows pay a large tax or be forced to marry again. By 1213, King John had collected so much tax that half of all the coins in England were stored in his castles.

The Battle of Bouvines

The reason for these high taxes was that John was desperate to win back his lands in France. He needed the money to pay for his army and weapons. In 1214 John and the Emperor of Germany agreed to attack France. Many of John's barons refused to join the invasion. The northern barons did not see what France had to do with them. John and the Emperor divided their attack. John invaded the south of France while the German Emperor invaded the North.

The plan nearly worked. Philip was almost killed fighting the German army at the Battle of Bouvines but, in the end, the French army won. John now had no ally and no hope of beating Philip on his own. He had lost the chance to win back his lands in France.

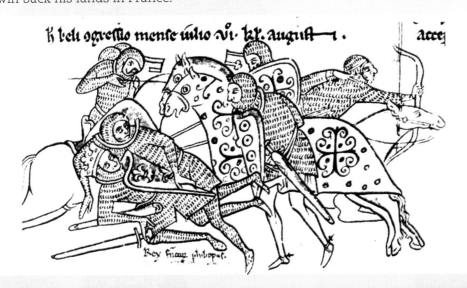

◄ A picture from a thirteenth-century chronicle of the Battle of Bouvines. It shows King Philip of France on the ground (you can see his crown). If Philip had been killed John would probably have won back his French lands and there would have been no rebellion in England!

Enquiry Step 4: Concluding your enquiry

It is time to use the work you have done in Enquiry Steps 1–3 to answer the enquiry question:

Why did the barons rebel against King John?

1 You now have five cards showing reasons why the barons rebelled against King John. Which ones do you think are the most important? Where would you put each card on the line below?

The least important reasons why the barons rebelled   The most important reasons why the barons rebelled

```
|--------|--------|--------|
1        2        3        4
```

2 Write your final answer to the enquiry question. Include all the five reasons, beginning with the reason you think was most important. Remember to include evidence to support your choice of the most important reason. Look back to page 54 for help in how to structure your answer.

How did the barons deal with troublesome kings?

John was not the only king who made his barons angry. Sometimes the barons believed they had to stop the king doing whatever he wanted even though they did not want to fight the king or start a civil war. On pages 60–65 you can find out how they tried to make sure kings such as John ruled England in the way that everyone expected.

The barons (who were also known as nobles) were the rich families who owned lots of land. In return for their land they provided soldiers for the king's army. They also helped the king by keeping their own areas of England peaceful and as free from crime as possible. The barons wanted to co-operate with the king and expected him to rule the country fairly. However, some kings:

- did not ask the barons for advice and just listened to advice from a few favourite advisers
- failed to lead the army courageously against foreign enemies
- let crime and disorder grow
- tried new and unfair ways of raising taxes for wars.

On pages 61–64 you will find out how the barons dealt with four troublesome kings – John, Henry III, Edward II and Richard II. After reading about each reign you will be asked to identify which of the options below were chosen by the barons as the way to deal with each king. Here are their options:

1 Force the king to agree to rules on how he should govern the country.

3 Depose the king and choose a new king. Ideally the new king would be a close relative of the old king.

2 Force the king to meet the barons regularly so that the king cannot do anything without their agreement.

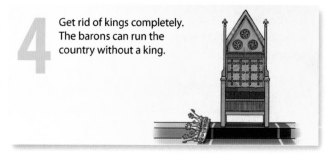

4 Get rid of kings completely. The barons can run the country without a king.

King John (1199–1216)

You have already (on page 59) worked out why the barons rebelled against King John but here's a quick reminder to get you started.

By 1204 John had lost his lands in Normandy to the French king. John's barons had many other complaints too:

- If barons did not send soldiers for his army, John charged those barons heavy taxes or put them in prison without trial.
- John did not trust his barons or ask for their advice but listened to a few favourite advisers.
- John quarrelled with the Pope over the right to appoint the Archbishop of Canterbury. The Pope excommunicated John and punished everyone in England by stopping all church services.
- John kept raising taxes unfairly. For example, he made barons pay massive amounts of money to inherit their fathers' land, ten times higher than they expected to pay.

The barons did not trust John any more. They gathered an army although they did not want to **depose** John. No king had been deposed since 1066 and people still believed that the king was chosen by God. In 1215 the barons forced John to agree to **Magna Carta** (the Great Charter), a set of over 60 rules about how the king governed the country.

The most important rules in Magna Carta were:

- The king should not demand taxes without the agreement of the barons.
- No one should be arrested or imprisoned without a trial.
- All the foreign mercenaries supporting King John had to leave the country.

A group of 25 barons were chosen to make sure that King John kept to Magna Carta.

Activity

1 Which of the four options on page 60 did the barons use to deal with King John?
2 Why do you think they chose that option rather than the others?

⬇ One of the four original copies of Magna Carta which still exist from the 40 copies made in 1215. Nobody knows what happened to the copy sealed by King John at Runnymede in 1215.

Henry III (1216–72)

Henry became king when he was only nine. While he was young Henry agreed to follow the rules in Magna Carta but it was a different story when he grew up. He was extravagant and untrustworthy. He only took advice from a small group of his wife's French relatives and he gave them rich rewards. Then Henry lent the Pope a huge amount of money for a war – without discussing the loan with the barons.

By 1258, the barons, led by Simon de Montfort, were determined to make Henry change his ways and keep to Magna Carta. They forced Henry to hold regular meetings (called parliaments) with them to make sure he governed the country according to the rules in Magna Carta.

However, Henry broke the agreement and this started a civil war. Henry was captured at the Battle of Lewes in 1264 and Simon de Montfort took over running the country. He called a parliament, inviting the barons and bishops who were on his side, two knights from each county and two merchants from each large town. He needed the support of as many rich men as possible in his war against Henry.

In 1265 Henry's son, Edward, killed de Montfort at the battle of Evesham. With Edward's help, Henry regained control of the country. When Henry died in 1272, Edward became king. Edward I was a great soldier and the barons were happy to follow him into war.

← Henry III's tomb in Westminster Abbey. Henry III was King John's son. He was very religious and rebuilt much of Westminster Abbey where monarchs are crowned and many are buried.

Activity

3 Which of the four options on page 60 did the barons use to deal with Henry III?

4 This was a different choice from the one made in 1215 under King John. Why do you think they chose a different option this time?

Edward II (1307–27)

Edward II was more interested in farming than fighting. He lost wars against the Scots, but the defeats didn't push the barons into rebellion. Instead they rebelled because Edward was only interested in the advice of his friend, Piers Gaveston.

On the day that he married the beautiful French princess Isabella, Edward spent all his time laughing and joking with Gaveston. In 1311 the barons forced Edward to send Gaveston abroad but they could not control the king for long.

Edward soon called Gaveston back, but the barons would not give up their fight. Their leader, the Duke of Lancaster, had Gaveston taken prisoner and executed. From that day onward Edward hated Lancaster. In 1322 Edward had his revenge when he had Lancaster taken prisoner and beheaded. This really angered many barons because Lancaster had not been legally put on trial. He had just been murdered on the king's orders. Five years later the barons (led by Roger Mortimer, the queen's lover) finally forced Edward to give up being king. His son (Edward III) was made king. Soon afterwards, Edward II was murdered.

← Edward II's tomb in Gloucester Cathedral. Edward II was one of the very worst kings in the Middle Ages.

Activity

5 Which of the four options on page 60 did the barons use to deal with Edward II?
6 This was the first time the barons had deposed a king. Why do you think they chose this option? (Think about how effective their choices had been with John and Henry III.)

Richard II (1377–99)

In 1381 Richard was the fourteen-year-old hero when he faced thousands of rebels in London and persuaded them to go home (see pages 88–89). Maybe this made Richard think he could do anything he wanted. But he made two mistakes. He made peace with France and then gave money and land away to his favourite advisers. The rest of the barons were angry that Richard was wasting money and not following up England's earlier victories against France. They rebelled in 1386 and took over running the country. Richard was furious but had to wait to take his revenge. Ten years later he struck. His enemies were executed or forced to hide abroad – but now it was their turn to want revenge. In 1399 Richard's cousin, Henry, returned from exile abroad with an army and forced Richard to give up being king. Henry became king. Soon afterwards, Richard was murdered.

← Portrait of Richard II dating from the 1390s which now hangs in the nave of Westminster Abbey, known as the Westminster Portrait. Richard became king aged ten after the death of his grandfather, the great soldier, Edward III. Richard's father, the Black Prince, had also been a great soldier.

Activity

7 Which of the four options on page 60 did the barons use to deal with Richard II?

8 Why do you think they did not choose the last option – to do away with kings completely?

So could medieval kings always do whatever they wanted?

What do all these decisions by the barons tell us? Here are some conclusions which will help you with this section's big question when you read pages 66–67.

1. Nobody wanted to get rid of kings completely

The barons tried a different way to get kings to govern the country properly. In 1215 they tried Magna Carta. In 1258 they tried parliaments. In 1327 (and in 1399) they deposed a bad king and chose another one. The new king was a close relative of the last one. The methods became tougher as time went on as you can see in this table.

John	Henry III	Edward II	Richard II
Agree to rules	Had to call regular meetings (parliaments)	Deposed	Deposed

However, the barons never got rid of kings completely. Nobody could imagine a country without a king because they believed that kings were chosen by God.

2. Rebellions only happened when kings broke rules

Rebellions only happened when a king did not ask the important barons for advice, gave all the rewards to his favourites and made the barons frightened he might attack them.

3. A king could do whatever he wanted – provided the powerful barons supported him

The king was still by far the most powerful person in the country. A king who had the support of his barons could do whatever he liked – raise high taxes, go to war – with no fear of rebellion. If the king was a great soldier and asked his barons for advice then they supported him. Barons and knights loved to follow kings like Richard I, Edward I and Edward III into war.

4. Ordinary people had little say in government

Parliament was not nearly so important as later in history. Parliaments first met regularly in the reign of Edward I (1272–1307) because he called Parliament to agree to taxes for his wars against France, Wales and Scotland. However, Parliament did not decide whether to go to war. Edward made that decision. Parliament continued to meet after Edward's death whenever kings needed money for wars and defence. However, if Parliament caused trouble, the king just closed it down. Ordinary people did not take part in Parliament.

Activity

9 Statements A, B and C below are all wrong! Explain why each one is wrong. Use examples from this chapter as evidence to support your explanations.

A Kings could always do whatever they liked in the Middle Ages.

B Barons liked to have a weak king who was a poor soldier.

C Barons were always keen to rebel against the king.

10 Why did the barons choose different options to deal with troublesome kings as time went on?

Could medieval kings always do whatever they wanted?

During Key Stage 3 you will explore The Big Picture of when and why royal power changed – from the Middle Ages all the way up to today. In this section you have begun to explore this big picture. These final pages summarise it – but we have left a gap we'd like you to fill in!

Part 1: Before 1066

Let's begin by going back before 1066 to the beginnings of the story of monarchy in Britain.

Activity

Look at boxes A and B.

1 Why were the reigns of Alfred, Edward and Athelstan so important in the story of monarchy in England?

2 What were the main tasks of the king at this time?

A

400–870AD After the Romans left Britain in around 400AD, the country split up into small kingdoms. Each had its own king who led his men into war with the kingdoms nearby.

B

870–1066AD England became united with one king for the whole country for the first time. The man who began to unite England was King Alfred of Wessex, when he fought back against the Vikings. During the 800s Viking invaders had beaten the kings in the North and Midlands and conquered most of England.

Alfred, the king of Wessex in the south of England, was the only king left to fight back. Alfred was a great soldier and he beat the Viking armies in the South. Over

ALFRED 870–99
EDWARD 899–924
ATHELSTAN 924–39

WESSEX

the next 40 years his successors Edward and Athelstan fought their way north and took control of the whole of England.

Alfred and his successors were the first kings to make laws for the whole of England. They saw it as their job to protect their people from crimes and violence. They also called council meetings of their most powerful lords to discuss laws and other important issues.

Part 2: 1066–1500

This is the part of the story you've studied in this book. The scenes below summarise two important parts of the story of the power of the kings in the Middle Ages.

Activity

3 Write a caption of up to 150 words summing up the story of royal power in these pictures (C). Use examples of successful and unsuccessful kings to add supporting evidence in your summary.

C

Some kings did this:

Other kings did not!

Part 3: After 1500

You will continue the story of the monarchy later in Key Stage 3 History but here is a peep into the future after 1500.

Activity

4 Look at pictures D and E.
   a) What continuities can you see with events in the Middle Ages?
   b) What happened that was different from events in the Middle Ages?

D

E

In 1534 Henry VIII changed the country's religion from Catholic to Protestant but he had to call Parliament to make his changes legal. Hardly anyone dared to say Henry was wrong. Those who did oppose him were usually executed.

In 1649 King Charles was executed to end the Civil War. His opponents in Parliament had not wanted to remove the king but it was the only way to end the war. Between 1649 and 1660 there was no king. England was ruled by the Lord Protector, Oliver Cromwell, until he died in 1658. In 1660 Charles I's son was recalled from exile to become King Charles II.

Did rats and rebels change people's lives completely?

Imagine you'd been born in the Middle Ages instead of the twenty-first century. What would your life have been like? This section will help you investigate what your homes, clothes, food and all kinds of other vital things would have been like. You'll also meet a lot of rats and some very angry rebels and find out what part they played in changing people's lives.

One of the hardest things for us to do is imagine what the medieval world looked like. It was very different in many ways. For example, there were no electric lights and no cars or tarmac roads. This reconstruction drawing gives you a good idea of what that medieval world was like. It shows the village of Wharram Percy in Yorkshire as it probably looked in the early 1300s. The drawing is based on evidence found by archaeologists.

Most people lived in villages like this. Each village had a lord who had been given the land by the king. Most villagers worked for the lord. Medieval villagers are often called 'peasants' which is another word for farmworkers. Try to answer the questions in the activity on page 69.

⬆ This illustration is a close-up of the church in Wharram Percy. You can see it near the top right of the main picture.

Activity

1 What kinds of work did people do in Wharram Percy?
2 What tells you the church was important to the villagers?
3 Who do you think lived in the large house shown at the bottom of page 68? Explain the reasons for your answer.
4 How clean do you think the houses were and what were they made of?
5 Which three words would you choose to describe life in Wharram Percy?
6 What three questions do you want to ask about people's lives in this village?
7 What kinds of sources do you think the artists used in researching this picture? Think back to your work on the Battle of Hastings (pages 26–29) to help you.

What can evidence tell us about the lives of medieval peasants?

One of the authors of this textbook recently asked his class to find out about the lives of ordinary people in the fourteenth century. They had to find out about the way people lived, worked and had fun. As you might expect, the students all rushed to get online! The email below gives you an idea of the kind of responses the teacher received from his class.

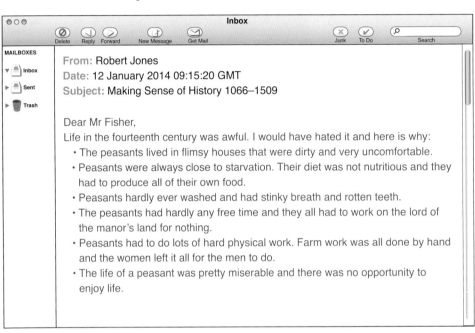

Inbox

| Delete | Reply | Forward | New Message | Get Mail | | Junk | To Do | Search |

MAILBOXES
▼ Inbox
▶ Sent
▶ Trash

From: Robert Jones
Date: 12 January 2014 09:15:20 GMT
Subject: Making Sense of History 1066–1509

Dear Mr Fisher,
Life in the fourteenth century was awful. I would have hated it and here is why:
- The peasants lived in flimsy houses that were dirty and very uncomfortable.
- Peasants were always close to starvation. Their diet was not nutritious and they had to produce all of their own food.
- Peasants hardly ever washed and had stinky breath and rotten teeth.
- The peasants had hardly any free time and they all had to work on the lord of the manor's land for nothing.
- Peasants had to do lots of hard physical work. Farm work was all done by hand and the women left it all for the men to do.
- The life of a peasant was pretty miserable and there was no opportunity to enjoy life.

Think

Look at picture A. What clues might historians and archaeologists find out about the lives of peasants from looking at their bones?

⬇ Part of the churchyard in the medieval village of Wharram Percy under excavation by archaeologists.

The author wants you to help decide what he should say in his feedback. To do this you will look at different types of evidence including bones, pictures and other archaeological and physical remains from the Middle Ages. This research will help you to correct the email and suggest changes. At the end you can write your own email summing up what life in the fourteenth century was really like.

Now it's time to begin exploring the lives of the people who lived in villages such as Wharram Percy using the evidence of pages 71–73.

A

What does evidence reveal about the work peasants did?

This page contains information on the work peasants did. The pictures come from the Luttrell Psalter, a prayer book made around 1330 for Sir Geoffrey Luttrell, Lord of the Manor of Irnham in Lincolnshire. The pictures show people who lived in Irnham.

B

C

⬆ Ploughing the land before seed was planted. The plough was pulled by oxen, showing how important animals were to peasants. In picture C, the people are breaking up clumps of soil to stop ploughs getting stuck in the clumps.

D

⬆ Harvesting was done by both men and women. Everyone took part – men, women and children. Corn was cut with a scythe or sickle, then taken away in bundles. Children picked up every last piece so nothing was wasted.

E

Peasants did not work on Sundays, saints' days and Church holidays like Easter and the twelve days of Christmas. They had more time off than many people today.

F

In 1300 around 40 per cent of villagers were **villeins** who had to work on the lord's land for one or two days a week without pay. They also needed to ask permission to leave the village and even to get married. However, this meant 60 per cent were freemen who paid rent to the lord and only did paid work on his land.

Activity

1 Look at evidence B–F. Decide which statements in the email on page 70 need correcting.

2 Correct the statements you have chosen. Here is an example.

> [at least as much]
> ∧
> The peasants had ~~hardly any~~ free time
> [as people today. The majority of
> peasants were paid for the work they did.]
> ~~and they all had to work on the lord of the
> manor's land for nothing.~~

3 Now add evidence to your statements to back them up. Use these phrases or come up with your own:

We know this because …

There is evidence to support this …

The evidence tells us …

What does evidence reveal about the lives peasants led?

Historians and archaeologists can learn much about the lives of peasants from studying their bones and the other physical evidence that they left behind.

G

This picture shows vertebrae (bones from the spine) from a man aged around 45 who died in the mid-1300s. Many medieval bone joints are worn smooth from lots of use and some show extra growth caused by damage. This was likely due to wear and tear. Skeletons also tell us that people's lives were much shorter than they are today. More than one in five babies died before their first birthday. Many women died in childbirth. Fifty was a good age.

H

It is clear from analysis of peasants' bones that many of them enjoyed fish in their diet, even in areas far from the coast. Fish was eaten on the many religious days when people were not allowed to eat meat. This suggests there were trade links with other towns and markets, which allowed peasants to purchase some of their food.

I

Archaeologists studying the remains of peasants' houses have been surprised at how well built these were. Many houses had stone foundations and most used expertly made wooden frames, suggesting that some peasants hired carpenters. The floors of many of these houses dipped from the continual sweeping.

J

Archaeological excavations have revealed glazed French pottery, wardrobes, chairs and even timber floors in the houses of some peasants.

K

Weather was important in the Middle Ages because it would affect how good the harvest was each summer. Too cold, too hot or too wet and this could spell hunger for the peasants. If the harvest failed for two or three years in a row, some people starved to death. Luckily this did not happen too often.

L

There is evidence of caskets and chests that could be locked with a key. This indicates some peasants owned items worth locking up.

N

The village church and churchyard were used for all sorts of events. These included feasts, fairs, puppet shows, archery contests and dances. There were also drinking parties known as church ales and mystery plays. Events like these cheered people up. The whole village could meet, share news and gossip.

M

The average medieval peasant would have eaten a daily diet of porridge, soup, two loaves of bread, 8oz (or 227 grams) of meat or fish, and vegetables including beans, parsnips and turnips. There were no biscuits, sweets, chocolate or foods containing high levels of sugar – so there was less tooth decay than today. The largest part of a peasant's diet was bread. The bread contained coarse grains and grit, which wore down teeth to a flatter surface. This made it less likely for food to get stuck and cause decay.

O

Although peasants did not have baths as regularly as rich people, they did use soap. This was made from boiling sheep fat in ash and caustic soda! They also used hazel twigs to brush their teeth.

Activity

4 Look at evidence G–O and decide which statements in the email on page 70 might need changing or correcting.

5 Change or correct the statements you have chosen. An example of how you might change one statement is given below.

              [did wash]   [did not have]
                  ^   ^
  Peasants ~~hardly ever washed~~ and ~~had stinky breath and~~ rotten teeth.

6 Now add evidence to your statements to back them up. You can choose some of the following phrases or come up with your own:

  We know this because …

  There is evidence to support this …

  The evidence tells us …

7 Now you have rewritten the statements in activities 1–6, put them together in an email send to your teacher to answer the question:

'What can evidence tell us about the lives of medieval peasants?'

What was the farming year like for peasants?

Most people who lived in England in the Middle Ages were farmworkers who are also called peasants. Everyone in the village had strips of land to work on. These strips were scattered so that the best land was not all owned by a few people. Even so, it was a tough life. Play this game to see if you could survive the peasant's year.

Activity

1 Work in groups of 3 or 4. You are competing with each other to see who ends the game with the most baskets of grain and therefore gets the most food. Each group needs a dice.

a) Each player starts the year with 25 baskets of grain to feed your family. If you end up with 25 you will have plenty of food. If you end up with less than 6, you will starve.

b) Take it in turns to roll the dice. Read the information in the table depending on the number you throw.

c) Each player needs to keep a record of how they are doing. Copy and complete the chart below. The first round has been completed for you to show you what to do. Do not copy round 1. It is just an example. When you have all completed round 1, move on to round 2, and so on until round 6.

Round	What happened	Baskets gained	Baskets lost	Running total (start with 25)
1 Land is given out	Strips of land are on very fertile land. Anything will grow	2	–	27

2 When you have finished discuss the following questions as a class:

a) Who had enough to eat? Why?

b) Who didn't survive? Why?

c) What has playing this game taught you about the lives of medieval peasants?

Rounds

Round 1: January–February
Land is given out by the Lord

Round 2: March
Preparing the land

Round 3: April–May
Sowing the seeds

Round 4: May–July
Growing the crops

Round 5: August–September
Harvesting your crops

Round 6: October–November
Storing your crops

1	2	3	4	5	6
Your strips are on very fertile land. Anything will grow. **Gain 2 baskets**	Your strips are too near to the river. The ground is marshy and crops won't grow. **Lose 15 baskets**	Your strips are spread too far apart from each other. You will be too tired walking to tend them well. **Lose 8 baskets**	You are very happy with your strips. They are close by and the land is fertile. **Gain 1 basket**	One of your strips is very stony. It will be hard to tend and hard for crops to grow. **Lose 2 baskets**	Your strip is near to your neighbour's strip – he is a good farmer and will help you. **Gain 1 basket**
You haven't looked after your wooden plough well enough. It breaks and you lose time with repairs. **Lose 1 basket**	You plough in a rainy week. Soil sticks to your plough and going is hard. **Lose 1 basket**	Your father was an expert ploughman. He taught you well. Your soil is well prepared. **Gain 2 baskets**	Your oxen are weak. You haven't fed them well enough. The ground isn't well ploughed. **Lose 1 basket**	Strong oxen make light work of the ploughing. **Gain 2 baskets**	You decide to plough in a cold spell. The ground is too hard to break up effectively. **Lose 1 basket**
The birds eat your seeds as you sow them. **Lose 6 baskets**	You are well prepared, your children scare the birds as you sow. Your seeds will grow. **Gain 3 baskets**	You accidentally drop your seeds and lose many of them. **Lose 2 baskets**	You break your arm whilst drunk from drinking ale. You don't throw well. **Lose 15 baskets**	You carefully sow your seeds and your scarecrow works to stop the birds eating them. **Gain 4 baskets**	You choose to sow on a windy day. The seeds are blown away from your strip of land. **Lose 2 baskets**
It was too cold in May but the weather has been better in June and July. **Gain 1 basket**	It has rained too much during the growing period. **Lose 3 baskets**	Perfect summer weather. Little rain and lots of sunshine. Cereals ripen perfectly. **Gain 8 baskets**	A thunderstorm and torrential downpour ruin many of your crops. **Lose 5 baskets**	It has been a long hot summer. Your cereal crops wither away. **Lose 2 baskets**	Good summer weather with some rain and lots of sunshine mean your cereals ripen. **Gain 4 baskets**
Your family work efficiently together and you gather the harvest well. **Gain 4 baskets**	You and your neighbour work together to gather in your crops. You are a great team. **Gain 5 baskets**	You drink too much ale when harvesting and ruin lots of good crops. **Lose 8 baskets**	Your scythe is blunt and your fork is broken. **Lose 3 baskets**	You discover that insects have eaten some of your crops. **Lose 4 baskets**	The weather is perfect in the harvest season. Hooray! **Gain 5 baskets**
Your barn is leaky and damp. Many of your crops go rotten. **Lose 8 baskets**	You spent last winter repairing your barn. It doesn't leak and is now dry. **Gain 3 baskets**	Mice and rats sneak into your barn and eat much of your harvest. **Lose 10 baskets**	You discover that beetles have infested your barn and have eaten some of your harvest. **Lose 5 baskets**	You regularly check your stored crops for signs of insects, animals or mould and stop any problems from developing. **Gain 3 baskets**	Your barn catches fire in the middle of the night. All of your crops are destroyed. **Lose all of your baskets**

Why were so many people buried at Charterhouse Square?

A

⬆ A worker examining a skeleton found underneath Charterhouse Square, London.

B

In March 2013, workers building the new London Cross Rail train line in London discovered something shocking underneath Charterhouse Square. Whilst digging below ground they stumbled across a group of twelve skeletons. Archaeologists were called in. They used pottery buried with the victims to work out when they died. It was roughly 660 years ago – in 1348. The skeletons were found lying in neat rows, 2.4 metres below the road. According to archaeologists, there could be up to 50,000 more skeletons buried nearby dating from roughly the same time.

In evidence B you found out that twelve skeletons were discovered underneath Charterhouse Square, and that archaeologists think that there might be 50,000 more skeletons there. This is such a large number of people to be buried at roughly the same time that we have to ask: Why were so many people buried at Charterhouse Square?

That's your enquiry question and by the end of page 79 you will have built up a clear answer to that question. We will continue your enquiry with some more evidence.

Enquiry Step 1: First evidence – asking questions

1 Look carefully at A. What do you think is happening in this picture?

2 Read B. It gives you some background information to picture A. Now explain in a sentence what is happening in the picture.

3 What questions do you want to ask about this discovery?

C

Nick Elsden, leading archaeologist from the Museum of London, said in March 2013: 'At this early stage all the evidence points towards the Charterhouse site being part of a fourteenth-century emergency burial ground.'

D

A chronicler from the fourteenth century wrote that [in London] they dug broad, deep pits and buried bodies together, treating everyone alike, except the most eminent.

The **Black Death** arrived in England in summer 1348. By the end of 1350, nearly two and a half million people had died out of a population of roughly six million. Map F records details provided by fourteenth-century chroniclers. These chroniclers, like other people at the time, called this disease 'the pestilence'.

E

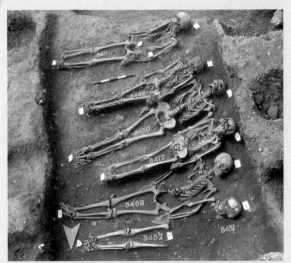

In nearby east Smithfield, a similar skeleton formation was found in the 1980s. A hundred skeletons were found, stacked five deep. Scientists discovered that the people buried here were killed by a disease known as the Black Death.

F

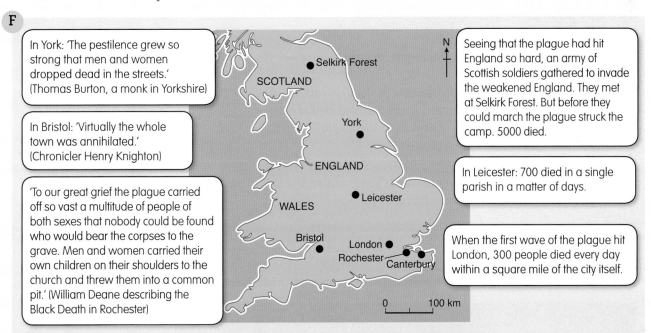

In York: 'The pestilence grew so strong that men and women dropped dead in the streets.' (Thomas Burton, a monk in Yorkshire)

In Bristol: 'Virtually the whole town was annihilated.' (Chronicler Henry Knighton)

'To our great grief the plague carried off so vast a multitude of people of both sexes that nobody could be found who would bear the corpses to the grave. Men and women carried their own children on their shoulders to the church and threw them into a common pit.' (William Deane describing the Black Death in Rochester)

Seeing that the plague had hit England so hard, an army of Scottish soldiers gathered to invade the weakened England. They met at Selkirk Forest. But before they could march the plague struck the camp. 5000 died.

In Leicester: 700 died in a single parish in a matter of days.

When the first wave of the plague hit London, 300 people died every day within a square mile of the city itself.

Enquiry Step 2: Suggesting an answer

Now you have looked at clues A–F (pages 76–77) it is time to think of possible answers to your enquiry question: Why were so many people buried at Charterhouse Square?

1 What is your possible answer (hypothesis)?

2 What evidence from A to F might support your answer?

3 You also need to show how certain you are. Where would you stand on the line of certainty below? Explain why you have made that choice.

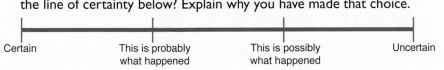

Certain | This is probably what happened | This is possibly what happened | Uncertain

You've worked out that the people were almost certainly victims of the Black Death. In the near future tests will be carried out on the skeletons at Charterhouse Square to try to prove this.

Now we can move onto the second part of this enquiry: Why couldn't they stop the Black Death from spreading and killing so many people?

Even now historians are not completely certain what the Black Death was, but it was probably **bubonic plague**. This disease is carried by rats and spread by fleas. A flea becomes infected when it bites an infected rat. It then passes the disease on to other rats and humans when it bites them.

People who had caught the Black Death felt tired and discovered painful swellings called buboes in their armpits and groins. This was followed by high fever and severe headaches. Blisters would appear over their bodies and most people died after a few days.

Enquiry Step 3A: Developing your answer

Clues G–M (pages 78–79) are all from the time of the Black Death. Use them to help answer the question:

Why couldn't they stop the Black Death from spreading and killing so many people?

1   Here are some possible answers:
   a   People believed God sent the plague so they spent their time asking for forgiveness.
   b   People knew the plague was caused by fleas on rats.
   c   People believed the plague was caused by poisonous air.
   d   People didn't understand what caused the plague.
   Or you could come up with your own answer.

2   What evidence from G–M might support your answer? You also need to show how certain you are. Where would you stand on the line of certainty? Explain why you have made that choice.

Certain	This is probably what happened	This is possibly what happened	Uncertain

---

G

Order to cause the human dung and other filth lying in the streets to be removed. This city is so foul with filth from out of the houses that air is infected and the city poisoned.

Order given from the king to the Lord Mayor of London.

H

◄ Flagellants or Brothers of the Cross, Netherlands, 1349. People walked through towns whipping themselves to show God that they were sorry for living sinful lives and asking him for mercy.

⬆ The king and **bishops** ordered church services to be held in every church at least once a day. In these services people prayed for forgiveness and asked God to put an end to the disease. Some people went further and made candles their own height and lit them in churches as an offering to God.

⬆ 'The Birth and Destruction of Saturn's Children.' The queen, in an elaborate bed, hands her newborn child to the king. The king is shown again throwing the child out of the window into a lake. Guy de Chauliac, a French doctor, blamed the Black Death on 'the close position of Saturn, Jupiter and Mars in 1345 … always a sign of wonderful, terrible or violent things to come.'

A Bishop suggested 'sometimes the plague comes from a toilet and corrupts the air. Sometimes it comes from standing water in ditches.'

You should avoid too much eating and drinking and avoid baths. Baths open up the pores of the skin through which the poisonous air can enter.

A cure given by John of Burgundy in 1365.

Medieval people thought people's bodies were being poisoned so doctors tried to draw out the poison. Here is a cure from a doctor's book.

The swellings should be softened with figs and cooked onions. The onions should be mixed with yeast and butter. Then open the swelling with a knife.

Enquiry Step 3B: Developing your answer

You have looked at evidence from the time of the Black Death. You should have an answer or a number of different ideas to explain why doctors could not stop the Black Death killing so many people. But before we draw our final conclusions, let's consider one last clue. Once you have read clue N think about the answer you have given to the question:

Why couldn't they stop the Black Death from spreading and killing so many people?

1 If you are now more certain that your answer is right, note down any more evidence from N that supports this.

2 If you think your answer may be wrong change it to a new answer and note down any evidence that supports this new answer.

3 How certain are you now? Where would you stand on the line of certainty? Explain your choice.

Certain　　　This is probably　　　This is possibly　　　Uncertain
　　　　　　what happened　　　what happened

N

Medieval people did not know about germs causing disease. They did not know that plague was spread by fleas and rats. Germs were discovered 500 years later with the use of microscopes. It was only then that scientists and doctors began to work out what caused the Black Death.

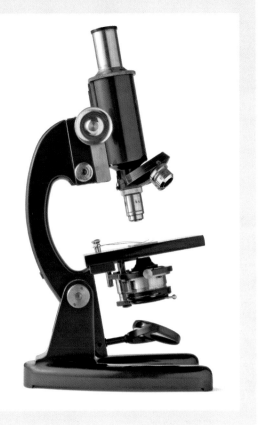

Enquiry Step 4: Concluding your enquiry

It is time to use the work you have done in Enquiry Steps 1–3 to answer the enquiry question:

Why were so many people buried at Charterhouse Square?

1   Try to include:
    ▮ what you think caused so many deaths
    ▮ what people at the time did to try to stop so many people dying
    ▮ why people at the time couldn't stop so many people dying.

2   You need to support your answer with evidence. The more precise evidence you use the better. Use the sentence starters below to help you if needed.

> I believe that the people buried underneath Charterhouse square died because …

> I think this because …

(Back up your answer with evidence from pages 76–77, Enquiry Steps 1–2.)

> So many people died because …

(Back up your answer with evidence from Enquiry Steps 3A and 3B.)

3   Use tentative language to show how sure you are of your answer, such as:
    ▮ definitely ▮ most probably ▮ probably ▮ possibly ▮ perhaps.

What else can the Charterhouse skeletons tell us about history?

Some people are surprised that we write new History books because they think that history never changes. They are wrong! History changes all the time because historians keep finding out more about the past. The Charterhouse skeletons, for example, have changed what we know about the impact of the Black Death in London. Archaeologists often find skeletons from all periods of the past and so we keep learning more about the height, strength and health of people who lived in the past. Later in this book (page 120) you will find out about a very famous skeleton discovered in 2012.

Historians also make new discoveries in documents. Many, many thousands of documents survive from the Middle Ages. For example, historians have been reading documents telling us about daily life in towns such as York, Ipswich and Southampton. History books used to say that people in the Middle Ages did not try to keep their towns clean and healthy. Thanks to new discoveries we now know that is wrong. We have discovered lots of evidence of people having fresh water piped into their towns, the streets cleaned regularly and waste taken away in sewers.

So, the Charterhouse skeletons remind us that history does keep changing because we keep discovering new things about the past. That's just one of the reasons why history is so fascinating!

Would you have joined the Peasants' Revolt in 1381?

It is Thursday 13 June 1381. Parts of London are burning. The city gates are wide open and the houses of many of the king's advisors have been looted. These advisers have locked themselves in the Tower of London but they still face death, as the picture opposite shows. What was going to happen to the king, Richard II, who was only fourteen years old?

This picture was drawn about ➡ 50 years after these events. It comes from a history of events in England and France written by Jean Froissart, a Frenchman, between 1381 and 1388.

This is not a war. England has not been invaded by a foreign enemy. Instead, ordinary people have joined a protest which will become known as the Peasants' Revolt. You are about to take on the role of a farmer from the county of Kent and make a series of important decisions. The most important one is: would you have joined the revolt?

The background to the revolt

You are an important man in your village, trusted by the other villagers. This year they've chosen you as the constable, to protect the village from crime. Of course this is on top of your work, farming your land.

You own enough land and animals to feed your family. You also work two days a week on your lord's land but he pays low wages – a law called the Statute of Labourers says you have to work for the same wages as 35 years ago, before the Black Death. After so many people had died, the survivors hoped they would be paid more because there were fewer workers. Instead the king and the nobles stopped wages increasing, unwilling to pay workers more money.

These low wages are not your only concern. Which of these issues in picture A would most worry you? Why?

A

> The French are attacking towns only 20 miles from where I live. The lords should be fighting to defend ordinary people in these towns but they are not.

> A new poll tax has been introduced: Everyone pays the same – lords and villagers. It's three times higher than the last one from 1379.

> The government has increased the tax I pay and has sent tax collectors into the villages to collect it.

> No one trusts the king's advisors: Simon of Sudbury (Archbishop of Canterbury who came up with the idea for the poll tax), John of Gaunt (who persuaded the young king to agree) and Robert Hales (the Chancellor who looks after England's money – my taxes!)

Activity

1 Now that you know the background to the revolt, you need to decide if you will join. At each Decision Point on pages 84–85 you will be given a set of options. Create a table like the one below to record what you decide to do. At the end you will be able to examine the consequences of your choices and learn what really happened.

To help you see whether your decisions have a positive or negative impact, you will gain and lose points. You start with ten points and will need to note down what you lose and gain as you read the Consequences section on pages 86–87.

Decision Point	What did you decide?	Consequences of your decision (start with 10 points)	What really happened?

Decision Point 1: Will you pay the poll tax?

Tax collectors are visiting every village. There's talk of people not paying the **poll tax**. What will you decide?

> 1 **Pay** the tax – that's 12 pence for you and 12 pence for your wife.
> 2 **Hide** – the tax collectors will never find people in the woods.
> 3 **Rebel** – attack the tax collectors to show how angry everyone is.

Decision Point 2: Tax collectors!

The government is angry at people avoiding paying tax by hiding. They're sending more tax collectors to punish them. Men in Essex have retaliated by drowning a tax collector in the village pond. Some people are talking of marching to London to present your case to the king. Maybe the king will sack his hated advisors and abolish the poll tax.

There's a meeting in the village. People will listen to you. What will you tell people?

> 1 **Pay the tax** and accept the punishment. If this protest doesn't work you'll all be punished.
> 2 **Hide again** – though the tax collectors are bringing soldiers.
> 3 **Join the protest.** It's an adventure. You've never been to London. If this protest works, you'll earn more and the villeins will be freed.

Decision Point 3: Slogan!

The protest is growing. The leader is Wat Tyler. He's trying to make sure people know this isn't a rebellion against the king. You have never met Tyler but have heard he is a good leader and a man to be trusted. What will your slogan be?

> 1 Down with the king and all lords!

> 2 For King Richard and the true loyal common people!

Decision Point 4: London!

London! Thousands of you are arriving from Kent, Essex and other counties. Even so, protesters like you are outnumbered. All kinds of people are joining in – criminals let out of prison, troublemakers, the London poor. It's getting chaotic. What do you decide?

> 1 **Go home.** It's dangerous to stay. Everything could go wrong.
> 2 **Stay** and make sure the protest reaches the young king. It's too important to give up now.

Decision Point 5: To loot or not to loot?

You see the luxurious Savoy Palace of John of Gaunt – the king's uncle and the most hated man in England. Gaunt's palace is being looted. One man is stealing silver, another is setting fire to the palace. What do you decide?

> 1 **Join in** and grab what you can for yourself.
> 2 **Tell** Wat Tyler so he stops the looting.
> 3 **Go home**. You never wanted looting and crime – you're a constable!

Decision Point 6: Do you believe the king?

This is what you've been dreaming of. Wat Tyler meets King Richard – and the king agrees to your demands. He will set villeins free, allow everyone to earn as much as they wish and he will think again about the poll tax. Wat is no fool and wants a signed promise. The king says he will bring one tomorrow. What do you decide?

> 1 **Go along** to watch and cheer?
> 2 **Insist** that Wat increases your demands – to get rid of all lords forever so that everyone is equal?

Decision Point 7: Will you attack the Tower?

The king's hated advisers have fled to the Tower of London. They have few guards. You have thousands of men. People in Kent particularly hate Simon Sudbury, the Archbishop of Canterbury, because he's a very harsh landowner. What do you decide?

> 1 **Attack** the Tower, take the king's advisers prisoner and put them on trial in a court. Then the king will see how law abiding you all are.
> 2 **Stay away** from the Tower. This violence is frightening the lords. They say you are rebels and deserve death.
> 3 **Attack** the Tower and **murder** the king's advisers.

Decision Point 8: The biggest decision of all!

Next day, young King Richard II at the head of 60 knights and nobles meets Wat Tyler but a quarrel breaks out. You hear the Mayor of London call Tyler a 'base knave' and strike him with his sword. Then a knight stabs Tyler. It seems as if he is dead. The boy king rides forward and says:

'Sirs, what is the matter? You shall have no other leader except me. I am your king. Be peaceful.'

He promises you will be granted all your demands if you go home peacefully. What do you decide?

> 1 **Shout 'charge' and attack** the king and his men. You will kill them easily because they're outnumbered. That's the only way to get what you want.
> 2 **Trust the king and go home**. Surely the king won't lie? This means all your efforts have been successful and you can go home to your children.

Think

Now that you have made your decisions it is time to examine the consequences. Turn to pages 86–87 to do so.

The consequences of your decisions and what really happened

Activity

2 Record the results of your decisions on your table from Activity 1 on page 83. Also note down what happened during the real revolt in 1381. An example of how your table can be completed is shown below.

Decision Point	What did you decide?	Consequences of your decision (start with 10 points)	What really happened?
Will you pay the poll tax?	To hide in the woods.	+1 point You've saved yourself some money. Running total: 11 points	Many people chose to hide to avoid the tax collectors.

Decision Point 1: Will you pay the poll tax?

1 Pay the tax – lose 1 point. You've not done anything to improve your life and it's cost you a lot of money.
2 Hide – gain 1 point. You've saved a lot of money. Lots of people hid – as many as one in three in many areas.
3 Rebel – lose 2 points. Dangerous! You don't know if anyone else will rebel. Rebels are executed – very, very painfully! If only more people would protest!

In reality: Many people chose to hide from the tax collectors.

Decision Point 2: Tax collectors!

1 Pay the tax – lose 1 point. You've not done anything to improve your life and it's cost you a lot of money.
2 Hide again – lose 3 points. There's not much chance of hiding this time and besides, you look a coward.
3 Join the protest – gain 1 point. You've not paid the tax and you've stood up for what you believe in – but there's a long way to go to be successful.

In reality: Most of the villagers chose option 3 and thousands now joined the protest.

Decision Point 3: Slogan!

1 'Down with the king and all lords!' – lose 4 points. This sounds like rebellion. Remember what happens to rebels – they're hanged, taken down, their stomachs cut open and their heads cut off. You are NOT rebelling against the king. You're protesting against his advisers.
2 'For King Richard and the true loyal common people!' – gain 1 point. Good choice. You have shown loyalty to the king while still reminding him that you are angry about the poll tax.

In reality: Slogan 2 was the one used in the revolt.

Decision Point 4: London!

1 Go home – lose 1 point. After all that effort? You'll still have to pay taxes!
2 Stay and make sure the protest reaches the king – gain 1 point. This protest is important. If you and your friends leave, then the troublemakers really will take over.

In reality: Most of the villagers from Kent and Essex stayed in London.

Decision Point 5: To loot or not to loot?

1 Join in – not a good choice. Wat Tyler threw the looters into the flames! He says you are here for justice, not theft. Lose ALL your points!
2 Tell Wat Tyler so he stops the looting – gain 2 points. The protest will only work if you stay organised.
3 Go home – 0 points. The protest is still important but maybe you're right by this time – things are getting out of hand.

In reality: Wat Tyler killed a looter by throwing him into the flames.

Decision Point 6: Do you believe the king?

1 Go along to watch and cheer – gain 1 point. You'll be able to tell your grandchildren about the moment the protest succeeded.
2 Insist that Wat increases your demands – to get rid of all lords forever so that everyone is equal – lose 3 points. A priest called John Ball has been telling people that there were no lords in the days of Adam and Eve. Some rebels agree but this wasn't what you were protesting about. This would be rebellion. This will get everyone's heads cut off.

In reality: Most trusted the king. After all, it was the advisers who were hated. People thought the king was being misled. The king promised to free the villeins.

Decision Point 7: Will you attack the Tower?

1 Attack the Tower, take the king's advisers prisoner and put them on trial in a court – gain 1 point. This shows you're not a wild mob – but it wasn't what happened!
2 Stay away from the Tower – 0 points. Probably a good idea for you but it won't affect what happens in the future.
3 Attack the Tower and murder the king's advisers – lose 3 points. This will make sure the lords turn against you.

In reality: The mob attacked the Tower. Robert Hales and Simon of Sudbury were beheaded and their heads were put on spikes on London Bridge.

Decision Point 8: The biggest decision of all!

1 Shout 'charge' and attack the king and his men – lose ALL your points. You have attacked God's chosen one. The king's nobles will now do anything for revenge and will try to destroy you all.
2 Trust the king and go home – lose 8 points. The king had lied.

In reality: None of your demands were granted. What happened next? You will discover on pages 88–89.

Was the Peasants' Revolt really a failure?

We left the Peasants' Revolt at a crucial moment. Wat Tyler had been stabbed and the king had asked the protesters to go home. What happened next?

Look at Picture A. What do you think is happening? It might help to think back to the work you did on pages 84–87.

A

The picture shows a fifteenth-century artist's interpretation of the death of Wat Tyler and the end of the peasants' march to London. With their leader dead the rebels went home. It seemed that the Peasants' Revolt had failed.

You are going to decide whether this interpretation is true:
Was the Peasants' Revolt really a failure?

Activity

To help you to reach a conclusion about whether the Peasants' Revolt was really a failure or not you will need to gather evidence.

I a) First make a copy of the ripple diagram on the right.
   b) As you read about the events following Tyler's death on page 89 make notes on your ripple diagram to show the immediate, short-term and long-term consequences.
      ▌ Immediate = anything that happened on the day Wat Tyler was killed
      ▌ Short-term = anything that happened in the days and weeks following the death of Wat Tyler
      ▌ Long-term = anything that happened in the years after the Revolt.
   c) Note down in red, evidence that the rebellion had failed and in blue, evidence that it was successful.

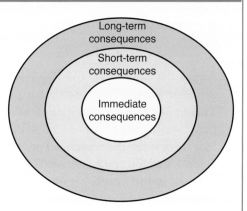

Long-term consequences

Short-term consequences

Immediate consequences

The king calms down the rebels. He tells them that if they return home peacefully their demands will be met. The rebel army heads back to the villages of Kent and Essex.

The king quickly raises an army which pursues the rebels, rounding up and executing their leaders. As many as 1500 rebel leaders are hanged.

The king goes back on all of the promises he made to the peasants.

Villeins you were and villeins you shall remain.

In the years after 1381 no further efforts were made by the government to collect the hated poll tax.

Wages for peasants slowly began to rise. Nobles realised that low wages would lead to more violence. By 1391 the government had given up trying to control wages.

Peasants became better off. They rebuilt their houses making them bigger and more comfortable.

Peasants could afford to eat more meat and began to wear more colourful clothes.

Because the Black Death had killed so many people there was a shortage of workers. This meant that lords could not keep demanding that people work for no pay. They could no longer stop them leaving the village. By 1500, there were no more villeins: all labourers were free.

Activity

2 Now that you have completed your ripple diagram you can answer the question:

'Was the Peasants' Revolt really a failure?'

Think about the following questions:

a) Have you got more red or blue points on your diagram?

b) How would you describe events immediately and shortly after the death of Wat Tyler?

c) How would you describe the situation for peasants 100 years after Wat Tyler's death?

d) What is your conclusion? Was the Peasants' Revolt really a failure?

Write a short answer in your notebook. Remember, as a historian it is important to support all of your arguments with evidence. Try to give examples of ways in which the Peasants' Revolt was a success or a failure.

Did rats and rebels change people's lives completely?

It's time to sum up the changes and continuities you've been investigating in this chapter. The rats that brought the Black Death and the rebels (though it's fairer to call them protesters) who stood up to the king and lords in 1381 did change people's lives in very important ways. If we'd been living in the fifteenth century we'd have been very grateful to them! But not everything had changed as you can see below.

Continuities in everyday life – what had NOT changed since 1066?

People's lives were still much shorter than ours in the twenty-first century. More than one in five babies died before their first birthday. Many women died in childbirth. Fifty was a good age.

Only 2 million people lived in England in the 1400s. Since 1066 the population had grown to around 6 million but then fell rapidly in the 1300s because of famine, the Black Death and frequent outbreaks of other epidemic diseases.

Nobody understood that bacteria (germs) cause disease. People believed God sent diseases as a punishment or they blamed the Devil or bad air or the positions of the planets.

Nearly everyone still worked as farmers. They still needed a good harvest to have enough to eat so there was always the danger of hunger. When there was a run of bad harvests between 1315 and 1319, people starved to death.

What had the rats and rebels changed by 1500?

Life does change. Things are much better than in our grandparents' days.

Opportunities for women

There were a lot fewer people so more workers were needed. This created more opportunities for women to do 'men's work'. More women ran their own businesses in towns. In Sheffield two women became blacksmiths. Women also married at a later age and many chose their own husbands instead of marrying a man chosen by their fathers.

Freedom!

By the 1400s everyone was free. They could move around the country to find higher-paid work. The lords could no longer control people's everyday lives.

Life was more comfortable

After the Black Death there were far fewer people to work in the fields. Eventually landowners had to pay higher wages to their workers to persuade them to stay, so many ordinary people had more money to spend. This graph shows how wage rates went up in the 1400s.

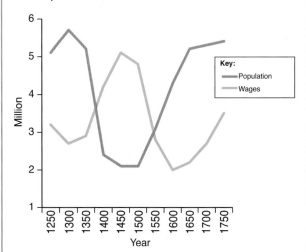

What did people spend their money on?
- Rebuilding warmer homes.
- More colourful clothing.
- More varied food – more meat and better quality bread.
- Schooling for their children. About half the people in London could read in 1500.

Activity

4   Draw your own version of the boxes on this page but summarise each section in no more than ten words.

5   Do you think that the changes were more important than the continuities in people's everyday lives? Choose one of the descriptions below and explain why you have chosen it. To help you decide, think about what would have been important to you if you had been living in 1500.
   a)   The changes were far more important than the continuities.
   b)   They were of roughly equal importance.
   c)   The continuities were far more important than the changes.

6   If we look ahead into the sixteenth century we'll see that the population began to grow. What effects do you think this had on people's everyday comforts? Look carefully at the section headed 'Life was more comfortable'.

Are medieval wars worth remembering?

These two pages were written on 11 November 2013 – Remembrance Day. Remembrance Day began after the First World War (1914–18) to commemorate those who died in the war. Since then people have worn poppies to remember those who died in this and other twentieth-century wars.

Most people think it is important to remember these recent wars because our parents, grandparents and other relatives took part in them. Family links make these wars feel very close and important. But should we also remember wars hundreds of years ago in the Middle Ages? That's the theme for you to explore in this section.

We'll begin by showing you which wars were fought in the Middle Ages and why they began.

Why did wars begin before 1066?

Before 1066 there were two reasons for wars involving British or English armies.

1 Britain was invaded many times before 1066 by Romans, Anglo-Saxons and Vikings. The Romans wanted Britain's silver and other precious metals, food and slaves to send back to Rome or to other parts of their empire. The Roman Conquest also increased the Emperor's fame and glory. Anglo-Saxon and Viking leaders wanted to take over land from the local British kings in order to become wealthy.
2 There were many wars within Britain. Local kings fought each other to win more land, power and wealth.

No British or English rulers were strong enough to send armies abroad to fight wars.

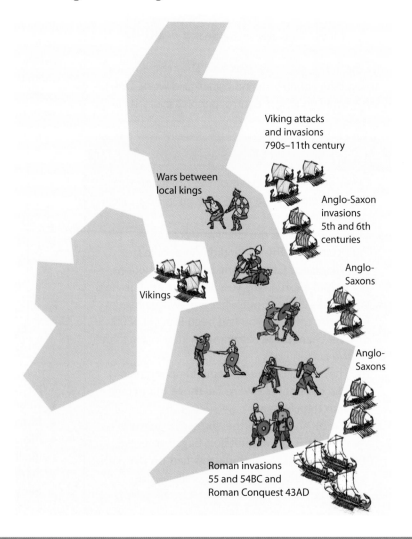

Viking attacks and invasions 790s–11th century

Wars between local kings

Anglo-Saxon invasions 5th and 6th centuries

Anglo-Saxons

Vikings

Anglo-Saxons

Roman invasions 55 and 54BC and Roman Conquest 43AD

Why did wars begin after 1066?

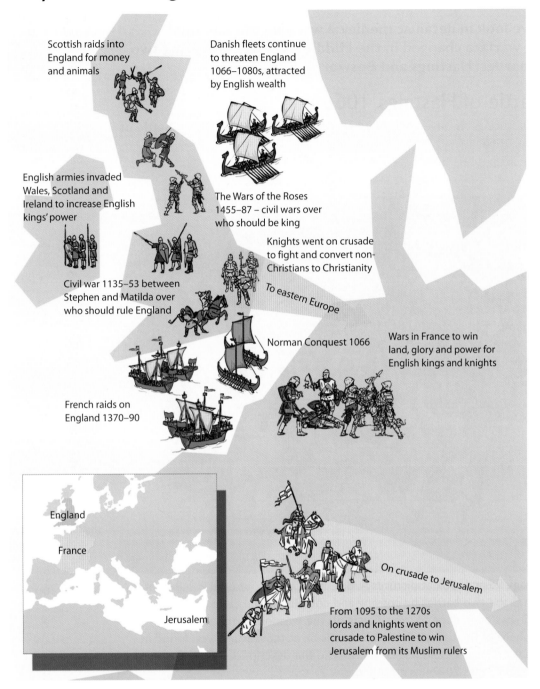

Scottish raids into England for money and animals

Danish fleets continue to threaten England 1066–1080s, attracted by English wealth

English armies invaded Wales, Scotland and Ireland to increase English kings' power

The Wars of the Roses 1455–87 – civil wars over who should be king

Knights went on crusade to fight and convert non-Christians to Christianity

To eastern Europe

Civil war 1135–53 between Stephen and Matilda over who should rule England

Norman Conquest 1066

Wars in France to win land, glory and power for English kings and knights

French raids on England 1370–90

England

France

Jerusalem

On crusade to Jerusalem

From 1095 to the 1270s lords and knights went on crusade to Palestine to win Jerusalem from its Muslim rulers

Activity

1 Why did people invade Britain before 1066?
2 Why did people invade Britain after 1066?
3 Why did English armies fight abroad after 1066?
4 Do you think any of these wars might be worth remembering? Can you suggest why – or why not? You can explore this question in more detail on pages 96–101.

Would a soldier from 1066 have felt at home at the Battle of Bosworth in 1485?

Before we look in detail at medieval wars we can find out whether warfare changed in the Middle Ages by comparing two famous battles: Hastings and Bosworth.

The Battle of Hastings, 1066

You saw picture A on page 24. It is an artist's reconstruction of the **Battle of Hastings** in 1066.

A

◀ A reconstruction of the Battle of Hastings by the artist Peter Dunn. You can see **cavalry**, lots of hand-to-hand fighting and a variety of weapons: spears and lances, chainmail armour, helmets, axes, shields and arrows.

Activity

1 Read page 95 and look at pictures A, B, C and D.
2 Compare the two battles by copying and completing the table below. One example has been done for you. Focus on the weapons, armour and the atmosphere of the battles. Remember to look at the features you found in picture A on page 24 and you could re-read the description of the Battle of Hastings on pages 20–24 as a reminder.

How was Bosworth similar to Hastings?	How was Bosworth different from Hastings?
Both battles had soldiers using shields for protection	

3 Use your table to write a sentence answering each of the questions below. Give reasons for your answers:
   a) Had warfare changed a great deal between Hastings and Bosworth?
   b) Did the similarities outweigh the differences?
   c) Which changes do you think were the most important? Why?

The Battle of Bosworth, 1485

The Battle of Bosworth was part of the civil war called the **Wars of the Roses**. It was fought between the armies of King Richard III and Henry Tudor.

Bosworth was largely a hand-to-hand battle between men on foot after the archers had fired their arrows. However, it ended with a cavalry charge when King Richard saw a chance to kill Henry Tudor. Sadly for Richard he was wrong. Minutes later he lay dead and Henry took the crown.

Thanks to the invention of gunpowder, the armies at Bosworth also used **artillery**. Cannon had first been used in England in 1327 but were still unreliable and sometimes exploded in the faces of the men using them.

B

⬆ An artist's impression of the Battle of Bosworth, 22 August 1485.

Changes in warfare

C

From the fourteenth century onwards, the **longbow** became the key weapon on battlefields. A skilled archer could fire ten or twelve arrows a minute over 280 metres. The longbow made cavalry charges very rare because horses were easily brought down by arrows.

Knights began to wear plate armour during the fourteenth century to protect themselves from longbow arrows. However, arrows could still punch through this armour.

A longbow man.

D

A fifteenth-century knight in plate armour. He is armed with a poleaxe. This had an axe blade and a spike which could drive through the weak joints of armour. A knight in armour could run, ride and get up if he was knocked to the ground.

Are medieval wars worth remembering?

> O flower of Scotland
> When will we see your like again
> That fought and died for
> Your wee bit hill and glen
> And stood against him
> Proud Edward's army
> And sent him homeward
> Tae think again

⬆ *Flower of Scotland* written by The Corries, 1965.

If you ever watch England and Scotland play rugby, the chances are you will hear the Scottish fans singing *Flower of Scotland*. Many Scots regard the song as Scotland's unofficial national anthem. Although it was written in 1965, the song deals with a battle that took place much earlier – in the Middle Ages – the Battle of Bannockburn.

Activity

In this enquiry you will act as a researcher for a TV documentary on three medieval wars and their consequences. You will decide how important each war was and how much time it should be given in your documentary.

1 Make your own copy of the table below to record your research on the consequences of each war. Begin by reading about the **Crusades** on page 97, then fill in the second column of your table. This has been started for you.

Think

Look at the lyrics of the first verse of the song above. What ideas do you have on what the song might be about?

	The Crusades	The wars of Edward I	The Hundred Years War
Changed the way wars were fought	Castles with square keeps began to be replaced with round towers and circular designs that were harder to attack.		
Changed the way people lived or thought at the time			
Created national pride or dislike of other countries			
Changed how countries were ruled or who they were ruled by			

The Crusades

In 1191, King Richard I (1157–1199) of England finally captured the town of Acre after a long siege. He showed no mercy and ordered the decapitation of 2700 Muslim prisoners. This act of bloodshed was just one of many by both sides in a series of wars that saw enormous death and destruction. However, there were many other consequences of the Crusades. Not all of these were negative.

England actually became a little more peaceful. With many knights away fighting there were fewer violent disputes at home. If a knight died on crusade and had no heir then his lands passed to the king. The more land a king controlled the more powerful he became.

> ### The Crusades
> **What:** Religious wars between European Christians and Muslims and other non-Christians
>
> **When:** Eleventh to thirteenth centuries
>
> **Who:** Many were involved but perhaps the most famous were King Richard and Saladin.
>
> **Why:** Christians and Muslims fought for control of the Holy Land, especially the city of Jerusalem.

The Crusades produced heroes on both sides. Muslims still remember Saladin (1138–93) as a brave warrior and excellent general who managed to defend Jerusalem during the Third Crusade. On the Christian side, King Richard I was praised as a fine example of **chivalry**. Both men even praised the other despite fighting on opposite sides. However, overall the Crusades led to growing distrust between Christians and Muslims.

A

Muslim scholars had made important discoveries in mathematics, chemistry and astronomy. This new knowledge was translated and spread quickly around Europe.

There were new ideas about buildings. Castles with square keeps began to be replaced with round towers and circular designs that were harder to attack. Churches also began to change, with spires and steeples appearing, perhaps influenced by the minarets (towers) used on mosques in the Holy Land.

The crusaders brought back expensive cloth and other luxury goods such as mirrors, silk, glass and perfumes. These became popular with those that could afford them and led to growing trade between Europe and the Middle East.

New fruits were introduced to Europe such as apricots, lemons and melons. Exotic ingredients like sugar, ginger and spices could be used to add flavour for those who could afford them.

What the Crusaders brought back with them.

The wars of King Edward I

Like the Crusades, King Edward's wars with Wales and Scotland caused much bloodshed and destruction. Soldiers raided villages on the hunt for food and supplies so whole areas were left deserted as a result, but these were not the only consequences.

Edward's wars in Wales, 1277–1283

Edward I further strengthened his control over Wales by sending thousands of English settlers to live there. Many Welsh peasants were evicted and lost their land and their homes as a result.

Edward gave the title of 'Prince of Wales' to his son. This tied Wales more closely to the English crown. From that time every heir to the English throne was given the same title. As we write this book, the heir to the throne is Prince Charles, also known as the Prince of Wales.

B

After defeating the Welsh, Edward ordered eight new castles to be built. These were hard to attack but easy to defend and so helped keep Wales firmly under English control.

King Edward built towns alongside his castles, which became important centres for trade, but only English merchants were allowed to do business there.

King Edward introduced new laws and taxes. English officials collected rents and imposed fines on anyone who broke the law or did not pay. This harsh rule angered many Welsh people and strengthened anti-English feeling.

⬆ An artist's impression of Conwy Castle around the year 1300.

The wars of King Edward I

What: Wars between England and Wales, then later England and Scotland.

When: Wales 1277–83; Scotland 1296–1304 and 1306–07.

Who: King Edward I against Llywelyn ap Gruffydd (Prince of Wales) and John Balliol and Robert Bruce of Scotland.

Why: King Edward I wanted to control Wales and Scotland. The Welsh and the Scots wanted to stay independent from England.

Edward's wars with Scotland

Edward's wars with Scotland were less successful. The Scots proved harder to defeat than the Welsh. William Wallace rebelled against English rule and defeated an English army at Stirling Bridge in 1297. He fell into English hands in 1305 and was executed. However, his memory was not forgotten and along with others, he became a Scottish hero and symbol of the fight for independence.

King Edward had failed to conquer Scotland and his son Edward II was a very poor soldier and leader. In 1314 the Scots led by Robert Bruce were victorious at the Battle of Bannockburn and Scotland remained a separate independent kingdom until 1603.

C

← This statue of Robert Bruce commemorates the Battle of Bannockburn.

Think

Look back at the lyrics of *Flower of Scotland* on page 96. Why do you think it is sung, especially when Scotland play England?

Activity

2 Use the information on these pages to fill in the third column of your table from page 96.

The Hundred Years War

The Hundred Years War

What: Numerous on and off wars between England and France.

When: They began in 1337 and continued on and off until the early 1500s. Henry VIII (1509–47) was the last English king to invade France as part of these wars.

Who: Many different rulers were involved, most famously Edward III and King Henry V on the English side.

Why: English kings claimed the right to the French crown but French Kings did not agree!

The **Hundred Years War** saw big changes in the way that battles were fought. Longer range weapons like the longbow and cannons were used to devastating effect. Longbows had a greater range and could be fired more quickly than French crossbows. As a result, knights charging into battle on horseback were no longer the most effective tactic because the horses were easily brought down by arrows.

Think

Look at the weaponry in picture D. How can you tell which side is which?

D

Activity

3   Use the information on these pages to fill in the final column of your table from page 96.

← An illustration showing the Battle of Crécy, 26 August 1346 in which the longbow was used to great effect.

The length of the Hundred Years War meant that it cost both sides a huge amount of money. In England, this meant the king regularly had to raise taxes. This could not be done without the agreement of Parliament, which meant that it had to meet more often. Slowly, Parliament gained more influence over how the country was run.

The war created heroes on both sides. Despite being heavily outnumbered, King Henry V of England defeated the French at the **Battle of Agincourt** in 1415, became a national hero and inspired a play by William Shakespeare. On the French side Joan of Arc, a young peasant girl, claimed to have had a vision from God telling her to drive the English out of France. Joan won several victories against the English before being captured and burnt at the stake. Her memory is still a powerful symbol of French resistance and independence.

Many English knights returned home very rich from all of the plunder they had taken from France. This money was often used to build fine manor houses and churches.

The Hundred Years War helped create a strong dislike between the English and French. This lasted right up until the twentieth century when both countries were united against Germany in two world wars. Before the Hundred Years War, English kings and their nobles had spoken French. After the war, they spoke English like the common people. The fighting helped to bring the people of England closer together. They were united by the glory of victories such as the Battle of Agincourt and their distrust of the French.

Activity

4 You have now recorded the consequences of each war in your table.
   Either:
   a) Look at your completed table. The more important the war, the more minutes it will need in the TV programme. Do you agree with the editor's proposed timings on the right? Explain why you agree or disagree and support your views with evidence from your table.
   Or:
   b) Draw your own pie chart showing how you would divide up the hour-long programme. Add notes to explain the reasons for your timings. An example is shown opposite.
5 At the beginning of this section we asked whether you think medieval wars are worth remembering.
   a) What do you think now?
   b) What are the main reasons for your decision?
   c) What have you learned from this enquiry?

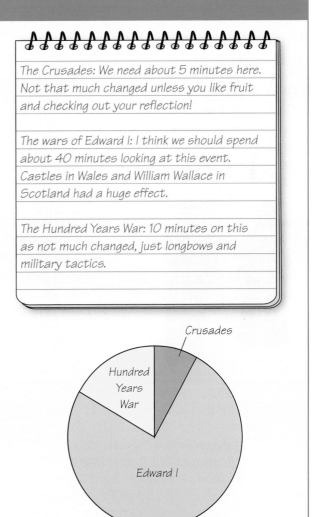

The Crusades: We need about 5 minutes here. Not that much changed unless you like fruit and checking out your reflection!

The wars of Edward I: I think we should spend about 40 minutes looking at this event. Castles in Wales and William Wallace in Scotland had a huge effect.

The Hundred Years War: 10 minutes on this as not much changed, just longbows and military tactics.

Crusades

Hundred Years War

Edward I

Was there a World Wide Web in the Middle Ages?

'Was there a World Wide Web in the Middle Ages?' probably sounds like a daft question! Of course not – there was no electricity, no computers, no 'www'. So why are we asking it?

Lots of people today think that medieval people did not travel and stayed in their home village or town all their lives. It is also easy to assume that the only contact medieval people had with people from other countries was when they tried to kill them in wars. But is this really true? Perhaps there was a World Wide Web in the Middle Ages. It couldn't have been through computers, but perhaps there *was* another kind of web linking people together. That's what this enquiry is about.

Did Britain have strong links with other countries?

Let's begin by exploring Britain's overseas links with other parts of Europe. Here are just some of the links from before 1066.

The Roman Empire

Britain was part of the Roman Empire for 350 years (from 43AD to around 400AD). During that time people from all over Europe and North Africa settled in Britain. DNA tests have proved that people living in Britain today are descended from people who came to Britain during the Roman period. Some would have been soldiers, some traders, some perhaps slaves. During this period many new ideas were introduced such as piped water and sewers in towns, bath houses and roads built from stone. Many British men joined the Roman army and went to fight and live overseas.

The Saxons

We do not know how many Saxon people came to Britain from northern Europe between 400 and 600AD. However, they changed Britain a good deal. They brought the language we still speak today and many of the names of our towns and villages come from Saxon words. Christianity also came to Britain in this period, brought from Rome by monks.

The Vikings

The Vikings settled in the north of England and Ireland in the ninth and tenth centuries (the 800s and 900s). They too brought their language which gave us many new words. As well as being warriors they were also great traders. They brought to Britain silverware, precious stones, jewellery, cloth, cooking pots, foods and spices from Russia, southern Europe and the Muslim countries of the Middle East and North Africa.

Activity

The cards below tell you about some of Britain's links with other countries. Your task is to organise them in different ways.

1 Sort the cards into two groups:
   a) Imported ideas – those which came into Britain and influenced people here.
   b) Exported ideas – those which were taken from Britain and influenced people in other countries.
2 Now look at the cards again. What other categories (groups) can you think of to sort the cards into? (The cards can go into more than one category.)
3 Look back to pages 39, 46–47, 48–49 and 95. What links with other countries can you find here?
4 Which import or development that came into Britain do you think was the most important? Explain the reasons for your choice.
5 How wide was the web linking Britain to the rest of the world in the Middle Ages?

A
Overseas workers brought skills such as brick making to Britain. Tattershall Castle in Lincolnshire was one of the first castles built from brick in the 1400s. A Dutchman called Baldwin was in charge of making the bricks for the castle – over a million of them!

B
In the 1470s William Caxton brought the first printing press to England. Printing had developed in Europe twenty years earlier. This meant books could be made more easily, so more people could buy them.

C
Many ideas about medicine and treatments came from Arab doctors. Their writings were used by doctors in England. They were translated into English in the 1400s to help people avoid new outbreaks of plague.

D
Wool and cloth made from wool were exported from England to Europe in huge quantities. These exports made many merchants and farmers wealthy and kept many English people in work.

E
In the 1490s the first voyages were made from Britain to the Americas. Sailors from Bristol may have been the first to make voyages hoping to reach new lands overseas.

F
Stone and glass were imported in large quantities to build cathedrals in England. Some of the best coloured glass came from Europe. **Masons** also travelled to and from Europe to lead the building work.

G
The stories of **King Arthur** are part of English history. Thomas Malory wrote the first stories of Arthur and the Round Table in English in the 1400s but he took many of the stories from books written in French.

H
English merchants imported a great many things from overseas – furs and timber came from north-eastern Europe. Wine, oil, fruit, silks and spices came from southern Europe.

I
The **Normans** brought the French language which added many new words into our language. These included names which became popular, especially boys' names such as William and Richard.

J
When the English lost their lands in France in the 1450s many English people had to come back to England. They sometimes brought their French servants with them who settled in England.

Why was there so much travel around the world in the Middle Ages?

Did anything on the last page surprise you? Perhaps you were not expecting so many links between Britain and the rest of Europe and some places beyond Europe. One reason we underestimate how much travel took place is because of **Christopher Columbus**. Columbus 'sailed the ocean blue' in 1492 and bumped into America by accident. It sounds as if no one had done much travelling before Columbus but that's very wrong. An earlier explorer was Ibn Battuta who was born in 1304 in Tangier in North Africa. Some of the places he visited are marked with red squares on this map – now that's exploration!

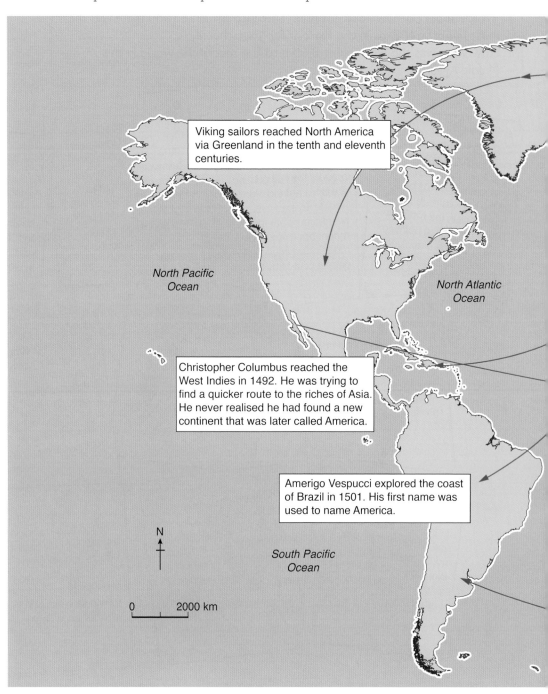

Viking sailors reached North America via Greenland in the tenth and eleventh centuries.

Christopher Columbus reached the West Indies in 1492. He was trying to find a quicker route to the riches of Asia. He never realised he had found a new continent that was later called America.

Amerigo Vespucci explored the coast of Brazil in 1501. His first name was used to name America.

North Pacific Ocean

North Atlantic Ocean

South Pacific Ocean

N

0   2000 km

Activity

Look at the map carefully.

1 What reasons can you find to explain the journeys shown on this map?
2 What evidence is there that Europeans were beginning to travel to more distant parts of the world in the late 1400s?

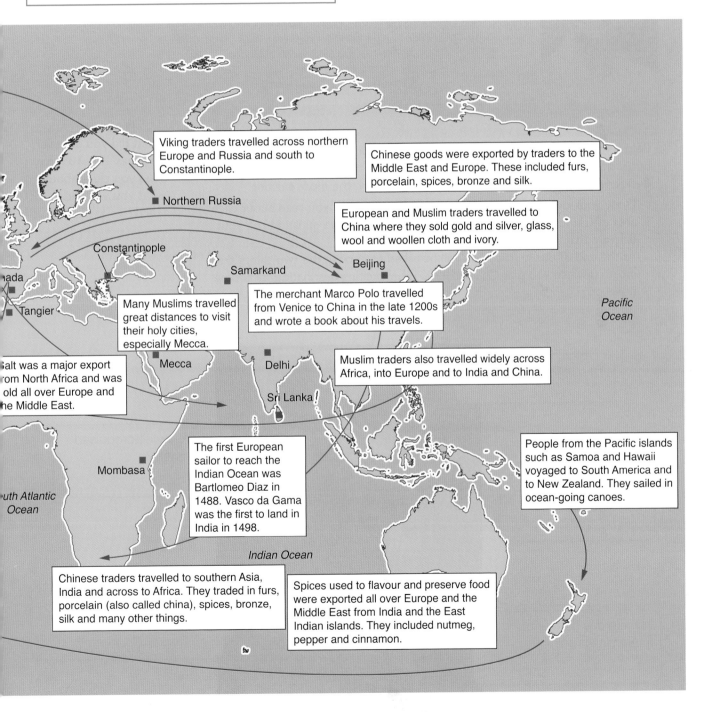

Viking traders travelled across northern Europe and Russia and south to Constantinople.

Chinese goods were exported by traders to the Middle East and Europe. These included furs, porcelain, spices, bronze and silk.

Northern Russia

European and Muslim traders travelled to China where they sold gold and silver, glass, wool and woollen cloth and ivory.

Constantinople

Samarkand

Beijing

ada

Tangier

Many Muslims travelled great distances to visit their holy cities, especially Mecca.

The merchant Marco Polo travelled from Venice to China in the late 1200s and wrote a book about his travels.

Pacific Ocean

Salt was a major export rom North Africa and was old all over Europe and he Middle East.

Mecca

Delhi

Muslim traders also travelled widely across Africa, into Europe and to India and China.

Sri Lanka

The first European sailor to reach the Indian Ocean was Bartlomeo Diaz in 1488. Vasco da Gama was the first to land in India in 1498.

People from the Pacific islands such as Samoa and Hawaii voyaged to South America and to New Zealand. They sailed in ocean-going canoes.

Mombasa

uth Atlantic Ocean

Indian Ocean

Chinese traders travelled to southern Asia, India and across to Africa. They traded in furs, porcelain (also called china), spices, bronze, silk and many other things.

Spices used to flavour and preserve food were exported all over Europe and the Middle East from India and the East Indian islands. They included nutmeg, pepper and cinnamon.

Why is China in 1300 such an exciting place to land your time machine?

Imagine that you are piloting a time machine. Its time controls are broken and you can only land in 1300 – in China! How do you feel? Excited? Frightened?

My name is Neil Bates, one of the authors of this book. I think it would be really exciting to land in China in 1300. I have spent lots of time in China over the years, learning Chinese Kung Fu and trying to understand Chinese culture. In the following pages I will explain to you why I think China in 1300 is such an exciting destination for a time traveller.

Activity

Below you can see the head of a terracotta warrior, a statue from an important burial site in the city of Xi'an. Around his head are criteria that will help you decide which aspects of Chinese life you think were the most exciting.

1 Draw your own sketch of the head and questions. As you read about each area of Chinese life write a sentence or two under the questions on your diagram that answers each one.

At the end of this journey you will be asked to choose the two things that most convince you that China in 1300 is an exciting destination for a time traveller.

Think

What did you discover on pages 104–105 that gives you clues about what you will find in China?

Will life be comfortable?

Are there advanced medical ideas?

Is there any danger of foreign invasion?

Is there a well-organised government?

Are people developing new ideas and inventions?

Are there advanced medical ideas?

China in 1300 had a depth of medical knowledge that England would not develop until the seventeenth century. Chinese doctors knew about the workings of the heart. Since the second century BC they had known about the circulation of blood in the body. They had removed blood vessels from corpses to investigate the distance travelled by the blood. In England, William Harvey did not make his theories on blood circulation public until 1628. The Chinese had also begun to experiment with a **vaccination** against the deadly smallpox disease centuries before Edward Jenner's first experiment in Britain in 1796.

These medical discoveries happened partly because Chinese medicine is based on a fascinating set of ideas and beliefs. The Chinese philosopher Laozi wrote a famous book called the *Book of Changes* in which he set out the ideas of a philosophy called **Daoism**. One of the ideas of Daoism is that everything in nature needs to be in balance.

A good example of this is the use of acupuncture which was commonly used to treat illness in 1300. The Chinese believed that illness is caused when the body is out of balance and the blood and energy (chi) do not flow smoothly. Acupuncture is where small needles are inserted into the body in order to stimulate and balance the flow of a person's energy.

A

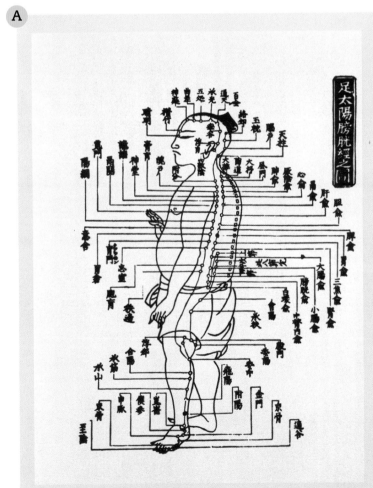

Fourteenth-century acupuncture chart showing the location of points into which needles would be inserted.

Is there any danger of foreign invasion?

For the discerning time traveller, medieval China had lots of spectacular places to visit. Some of those sights are still famous today. One of them, the Great Wall, was designed and built to protect the northern borders of China from the threat of Mongol invasion. It marked the border with Mongolia. The gates in the wall also served as check points for goods entering China along the Silk Road (a trade route transporting goods between China and the Middle East). The Great Wall is over 20,000 km in length. Made of stone and clay, it stands higher than a double decker bus. It has watch towers every 200 metres where warning fires could be lit to warn of enemies approaching.

> **Think**
>
> What does the size of the Great Wall tell you about the skills and organisation of the Chinese?

B ⬇ The Great Wall of China

Is there a well-organised government?

Another site, still visited by tourists today, dates from around 210BC and is the giant underground tomb of the Qin (pronounced 'Chin') Emperor near the modern city of Xi'an. This vast site is clear evidence of just how powerful and well organised the government of the Chinese emperor could be.

In 1974, farmers digging a well uncovered a life-sized clay soldier. Archaeologists moved in and uncovered thousands of terracotta warriors standing guard over the emperor's tomb. The warriors had weapons, armour and horses. More impressively perhaps, each clay warrior had an individual face. Other parts of the tomb contained figures of court officials, acrobats, strongmen and musicians. The tomb itself was said to contain a map of China with moving rivers of mercury and traps to stop tomb robbers.

The Great Wall and the terracotta warriors provide good evidence that the country was well protected and that it had strong and stable government. The Emperor was seen as an almost god-like figure. To help the Emperor rule the country there was a huge civil service. This had officials all over China in charge of collecting taxes, keeping detailed written records and keeping law and order. At the same time the Emperor had a navy, an army of over 1 million soldiers and he could communicate with his officials using the Imperial postal service.

> **Think**
>
> What does Emperor Qin's tomb tell you about his power?

C

⬆ Terracotta sculptures depicting the armies of Qin Shi Huang, the first Emperor of China. They were buried with the Emperor in his tomb to protect him in the afterlife.

Will life be comfortable?

China certainly had some great cities in 1300. One of these, Hangzhou, was allegedly visited by the Italian explorer Marco Polo in 1275, who described it as 'beyond dispute the finest and the noblest in the world'. Here is his description of Hangzhou.

D

The city of Hangzhou was well supplied with food: vegetables from the gardens and markets of the eastern suburbs and rice from the north. Food and other goods were carried into the city by canal. People and goods also moved around the city by horse and on **sedan chairs**. The city had many shops and restaurants, many of which were open all night.

There were shops for almost everything in Hangzhou. Some shops were for practical repairs of everything from ovens to knife sharpeners. There were stores full of luxury goods that had been imported from India and the Middle East; and other shops selling everything from noodles, fruit, thread, incense, to candles, oil, soy sauce, fish, pork and rice. If you needed entertainment in the streets you would find storytellers, acrobats, dancing, shadow-play, jugglers, puppets and musicians.

Think

Do you think that it would be possible to live comfortably in China in 1300?

Are people developing new ideas and inventions?

There were lots of other aspects of China in 1300 that would have been uncommon or even unheard of in medieval England. These included paper money, fireworks, the wheelbarrow, the umbrella, the printing press, the compass, tea, toilet paper and guns.

F

← Thanks to the invention of the printing press the Chinese began to use paper money (called 'flying money' as the wind could whip it out of your hand), about 500 years before the English.

E

← Red pavilion and gardens at the edge of West Lake, Hangzhou.

G

The Chinese first developed gunpowder in the tenth century. It was first used in battle in 1232 when 'arrows of flying fire' were used to stop a Mongol invasion of China.

H

The compass was first developed around 500 BC and was quickly adopted for the art of Feng Shui. This was a method of building palaces so that energy would flow through the buildings bringing health and happiness to the people who lived there. By 1000 AD compasses were being widely used for navigation by the Chinese navy.

I

◀ The Chinese have been drinking tea for over 4000 years. It was initially drunk as a medicine and then later became a regular part of Chinese life. Modern scientists believe that Chinese green tea is good for your health, for example helping people with high blood pressure.

Think

Would you rather land your time machine in China in 1300 than in England where you would need to wait hundreds of years for the inventions shown in pictures F–J to arrive?

Activity

2 Let's go back to the head of our terracotta warrior on page 106. You should now have an example for all of the questions around his head. Which two things would you have found most exciting if you had landed your time machine in fourteenth-century China? Write your two choices into your notebook and give reasons for your choices.

8

What can Anne Herbert tell us about life during the Wars of the Roses?

What can Anne Herbert tell us about life during the Wars of the Roses?

Imagine you could meet someone who lived through the Wars of the Roses. Anne Herbert did just that. She was born in 1433 and died about 1486. Sadly she did not write down her story but we have used detailed research to imagine what she would have told us about her family and her life. So sit back and find out what Anne can tell us about her life during the Wars of the Roses!

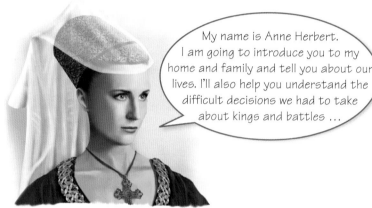

My name is Anne Herbert. I am going to introduce you to my home and family and tell you about our lives. I'll also help you understand the difficult decisions we had to take about kings and battles ...

I'll begin with my grandfather, Walter Devereux. He was one of the heroes who fought alongside Henry V in the wars against France. That's King Henry in the picture opposite. He was a great king. He made sure everyone kept the law. Two knights had a quarrel that led to murders until King Henry summoned them to meet him. He ordered them to sort out their quarrel before he'd finished the meal he was eating – or they'd both be executed. The quarrel ended!

King Henry was also a great soldier. My grandfather was there on St. Crispin's Day in October 1415 when we won the **Battle of Agincourt**. We only had 7000 men, many sick and exhausted after a long march. The French had

⬆ King Henry V (1413–22).

The kings and battles of the Wars of the Roses

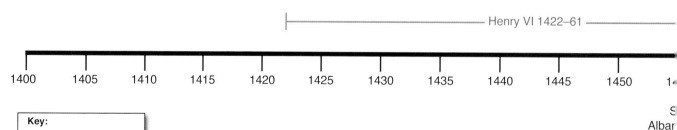

Henry VI 1422–61

| 1400 | 1405 | 1410 | 1415 | 1420 | 1425 | 1430 | 1435 | 1440 | 1445 | 1450 |

S
Albar

Key:
— Lancastrian dynasty
— Yorkist dynasty
— Tudor dynasty

twice as many men and expected an easy victory – but they didn't know about the greatness of our king. First every one of our archers poured ten arrows a minute into the French **cavalry**, stopping their charge – dead. Then King Henry led his men in hand-to-hand fighting, shattering the rest of the French army. We had won, thanks to God, King Henry and our **longbows**!

King Henry then conquered northern France. That's when my grandfather was killed attacking a French town. In 1420 the French agreed that King Henry would be the next King of France. We English had conquered France just like William of **Normandy** conquered England centuries ago.

Then King Henry died aged only 35. The new king was his nine-month-old son, also called Henry – Henry VI. The nobles ruled England for the boy king and we stayed victorious in France – until our new King Henry grew up. That's when everything went wrong.

We lost our lands in France and battles began in England. Since then the royal families of Lancaster and York have been fighting over who should be king. There have been far too many battles. That is why some people say this fifteenth century is a terrible time to live. They say that:

- People are poor and miserable because of all the battles in England.
- The nobles are not loyal to the king any more.
- The nobles keep rushing into fighting wars because they are greedy for power and wealth.

But I don't agree, even though my family has had some tragic times. I am going to show you what it's really been like to live during these wars. Then you can decide whether you think this is really such a terrible time to live.

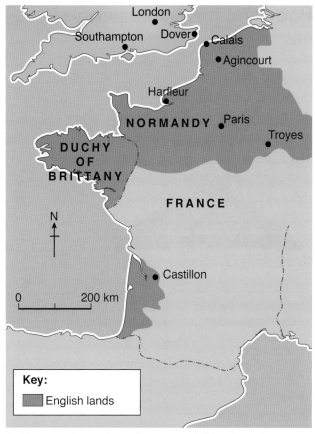

⬆ The map shows (in red) how much French land was conquered by the English by 1429.

Activity

1 Why did Anne believe that Henry V was such a great king?
2 Why was she proud of her grandfather?
3 What went wrong when Henry VI grew up?
4 Look at the timeline. Why might you think that:
   a) people were no longer loyal to kings?
   b) the nobles were always eager to fight battles?

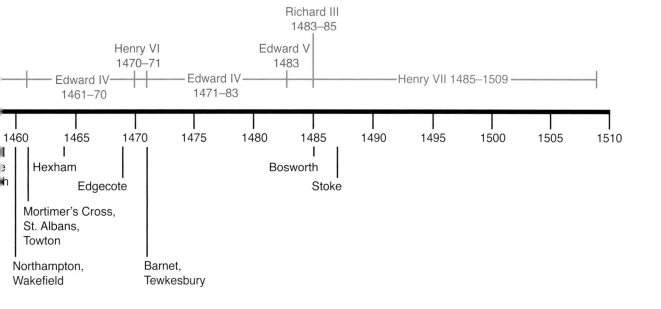

Poor and miserable people?

Welcome to my home, Raglan Castle in the borderlands with Wales. My husband, William, and I have spent a great deal of money rebuilding the castle. Do you think we look poor and miserable?

We rebuilt the castle to make it much more comfortable and luxurious. William was the Earl of Pembroke after all, one of the most powerful men in the kingdom.

Everyone is wearing the latest fashions – head-dresses, expensive furs and jewellery.

The battlements are really for show, not for warfare. We don't expect Raglan to be attacked. There are many other comfortable castles like ours. The only castles being built for war are on the border with Scotland.

The large glass windows make the family rooms and rooms for important guests much lighter.

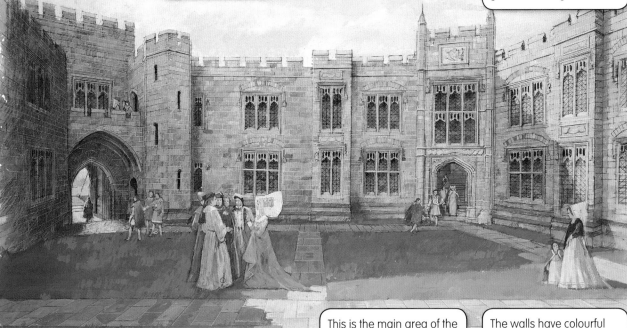

↑ A reconstruction drawing of Raglan Castle in the 1460s.

Outside you can explore our gardens, the deer park and the orchards full of fruit trees. And we have well-stocked fishponds to keep us well supplied with fish for meals.

This is the main area of the castle. There is another courtyard to the right where you'll find the kitchens, servants' quarters and all the storerooms.

The walls have colourful tapestries on them. Good for warmth and the pictures on the tapestries tell interesting stories.

We are lucky because we are one of the richest families in the country. But many common people also live more comfortably than their grandparents in the 1300s.

The great pestilence – you may call it the **Black Death** – was 100 years ago but it is still hard to find enough workers. We pay people higher wages to keep them working for us and so they are better-off. They spend their money on better food and clothes. They eat a lot more meat and have more colourful clothes. Many wear furs that used to be just for the rich. They have also built stronger, larger houses with more furniture, and better plates and dishes.

Have we been badly affected by the wars? That depends on who you are. There have been many years when there's been no fighting – look at the list of battles on pages 112–113. But people kept worrying. We often thought that the fighting had ended but then it started again. Not knowing what would happen next was almost the worst part.

A good example was back in 1461. Londoners were very scared when they heard the Lancastrian army was marching south, stealing food and looting. Everyone had heard how the town of Ludlow had been looted in 1459 when the Lancastrian soldiers got drunk. Happily they were stopped before they got to London. But it had been a truly frightening few weeks.

The part that really was the worst was waiting to hear if our loved ones had survived a battle. Thousands of men have died and each death affects family and friends. The lords and their men have suffered most. The common folk in the villages and towns have not been affected nearly so much. They have been able to get on with their normal lives.

Activity

5 What is Anne's opinion about life in the fifteenth century?
6 List three pieces of evidence she uses to support her opinion about
   a) her own family being well off
   b) many common folk being better off.
7 In what ways did the wars affect people's lives?
8 Do you agree with Anne that this was a good time to live or do you think the wars made people poor and miserable?

8

What can Anne Herbert tell us about life during the Wars of the Roses?

Did the nobles still want to be loyal to the king?

Now I'd like to tell you about the wars that have made some people believe that the nobles kept rushing into fighting **civil wars** because nobody was loyal to the king any more. My husband and my brother were two of those nobles. Let me tell you about the decisions they faced and then you can decide what you would have done in their place.

The disasters of Henry VI

On the right is Henry VI who became king when he was a baby. I first saw Henry much later when he was about 30. He was tall and broad and could have made a good soldier. Henry looked like a king should, but he didn't behave like a king. He was more like a timid priest than a soldier. A king has to punish criminals, but Henry hated to punish anyone. A king has to lead and inspire his army, but Henry was not interested in weapons or warfare. When there was a rebellion in 1450 Henry ran away instead of standing up to the rebels.

So our problems in England began because Henry was such a poor king. By the 1450s:

⬆ Henry VI, king from 1422 to 1461 and again briefly in 1470–71.

- We had lost all our lands in France. It was shameful to see English **refugees** from France arriving in London, pushing carts piled with belongings from their homes in France.
- There was more and more law-breaking. Powerful men knew they could attack their neighbours and steal belongings and land. The king would not do anything to stop them.
- Henry was often ill. Once he fell into a coma that lasted eighteen months and could not speak or understand what was said to him. He never recovered properly and always seemed ill.

1461 – who should we fight for?

Without a good king, quarrels and feuds broke out between the nobles. The first battle was in 1455, though, thank goodness, that was about who should be the king's chief adviser, not about who should be king. Then war broke out with a vengeance in 1459. There were six battles in eighteen months. My husband William and my brother Walter had to decide who to fight for. They could fight for the king, Henry VI of Lancaster, or for a man we knew well, Edward, Duke of York. Our family had served the Dukes of York for over twenty years.

William and I had six children so we had to be careful. If we lost our lands and wealth what would become of the children? Here are the choices we had:

Choice 1: Fight for Edward of York and make him king instead of Henry

Edward was eighteen years old, tall, handsome and already a great soldier. He looked like a real king, very different from Henry. He was one of King Henry's closest relatives. He said his family should have been kings since Richard II had been deposed in 1399. Edward also had the support of the Earl of Warwick, the most powerful nobleman in the country.

Choice 2: Fight for Henry and keep him as king

Most nobles were still loyal to Henry and would fight on his side. They still supported him because they believed he had been chosen by God to be king. If we fought for Edward and lost, then our families would lose everything – homes, wealth, and the men would lose their lives.

Choice 3: Stay at home and not fight

This would be the easy choice but we are important landowners. Having land and riches makes us responsible for solving England's problems. We need to take part.

⬆ Edward of York who challenged Henry VI in 1461. Sadly none of the portraits of Edward show how handsome and charming he was! He was also quick-thinking. At the battle at Mortimer's Cross in 1461 three suns were seen in the sky. Edward's soldiers were frightened but Edward inspired them by saying that the three suns were a sign that God was on his side.

Activity

9 What was the strongest reason for fighting for Edward?
10 What was the strongest reason for fighting for Henry?
11 Who do you think most nobles chose to fight for?
12 What would you have chosen if you had been a member of Anne's family?
13 Henry had been a terrible king since he was sixteen. That was 24 years of being a failure before he was deposed. Anne said that many people believe that 'the nobles are not loyal to the king any more'. Do you agree that the nobles were no longer loyal to the king in 1461? Give two reasons for your answer.

8

What can Anne Herbert tell us about life during the Wars of the Roses?

Did the nobles rush into fighting wars because they were greedy for power and wealth?

What did we decide in 1461?
William and Walter fought for Edward of York, firstly at Mortimer's Cross and then in that terrible battle in the snow at Towton in Yorkshire. Edward won a great victory and became King Edward IV. Henry fled but was eventually captured and imprisoned. Our new king Edward rewarded us well for our support. He made my husband William a lord – Lord Herbert. The king also gave William many lands and we became very wealthy. My brother Walter became a lord too.

Later William was promoted again to be Earl of Pembroke. We also looked after a very important young nobleman, Henry Tudor, who we hoped would marry our daughter Maud. He was only four when he came to live with us at Raglan and stayed until he was thirteen.

But then tragedy struck. In 1469 the Earl of Warwick turned traitor and rebelled against King Edward. Warwick was selfish. He wanted more power for himself, to rule the country by turning King Edward into his puppet king. Later he even made old King Henry king again for a few months. Warwick didn't care what happened to other people as long as he had power.

My husband, William, led an army against Warwick but was beaten. Warwick had William executed. We buried William in beautiful Tintern **Abbey**. I promised then never to marry again and I have worn black ever since.

I was delighted when King Edward killed Warwick in battle. Soon afterwards King Henry died in **the Tower**. He was probably murdered on Edward's orders, but I was not sorry. Now England could be peaceful – or so we thought. We did have twelve years of peace, then came events that were even more shocking than anything that had gone before.

1485 – Should we fight for Richard III or Henry Tudor?

King Edward died in April 1483. We all expected his twelve-year-old son to be crowned Edward V but, within three months, the young king's uncle Richard became king instead. Young Edward V and his brother were never seen again. Many people believed that Richard had killed the boys even though they were his own nephews. Several of the young king's supporters were also executed without a trial on Richard's orders. Many people were horrified by this sudden violence.

That was why a rebellion broke out. Many men, especially in the South, rebelled against Richard even though they were putting their lives, their wealth and their families at risk. They chose Henry Tudor as their new leader – the young boy I had cared for at Raglan back in the 1460s. They wanted him to be the next king of England.

This time it was my sons, William and Walter (we do like these names in my family!), who had to decide who to fight for. And my brother Walter, too, though he was now 50 years old. Here are the arguments we had to think about.

Why fight for Richard III?

- Richard is an excellent soldier.
- He has lots of loyal support in the North.
- Nobody knows Henry Tudor and whether he will make a good king.
- Richard did a good job of ruling the North while his brother was king.
- Richard says he is the rightful king because the boys who disappeared were **illegitimate**.
- My son William is married to King Richard's daughter.

← Richard III.

Why fight for Henry Tudor?

- My sons grew up with Henry at Raglan.
- A lot of southern knights support Henry, though we don't know how many more will support him when he invades England.
- Henry has been given ships and men by the King of France to help his invasion.
- Many people believe Richard killed his nephews because he wanted the power and wealth of being king. He also executed lords who might have stopped him becoming king.

↑ Henry Tudor as a young man.

Activity

14 What were the two strongest reasons for fighting for Richard?

15 What were the two strongest reasons for fighting for Henry?

16 What side would you have chosen if you had been a member of Anne's family? (Think about their family links, too.)

8

What can Anne Herbert tell us about life during the Wars of the Roses?

What did we decide in 1485?

Henry Tudor landed in Wales and invaded England in 1485. His army beat King Richard at the Battle of Bosworth. King Richard was killed. More importantly for us, my brother was killed fighting for King Richard.

Happily my sons survived because they did not take part in the battle. My elder boy, William, did not fight at all. To be honest, he was never a good soldier. My younger son, Walter, had been ordered by King Richard to stop Henry Tudor but instead he watched as Henry's army marched into England. I think he was close to joining Henry but decided to stay safe. Both my sons remember how their father was executed after losing in battle.

Discovering King Richard

After Richard's death at Bosworth his body was hastily buried in an abbey in Leicester but until 2012 nobody knew exactly where he'd been buried. Then archaeologists found his grave and used DNA tests to prove that the skeleton is Richard III. They discovered that:

- Richard had been killed by sharp blows to his head, perhaps from a poleaxe (see page 95).
- His spine was severely curved from a disease called scoliosis. One of his shoulders would have been higher than the other.
- After he died Richard's body had been mutilated and he'd been buried with his hands tied behind his back.

Think

Why do you think Richard's body had been badly treated?

Are our problems over?

← Henry VII (1485–1509) later in his life. This portrait was painted around 1505 when Henry was 48.

It's hard to believe that Henry Tudor, the boy who grew up with us at Raglan, is now King Henry VII. Recently he asked me to travel to London to meet him. He was very grateful for my care in bringing him up, called me his 'gracious cousin' and said many kind things.

But I am not sure Henry will be a good king. It should be an easy task to unite the nobles as nearly everyone wants peace after so many deaths. We want a king we can be loyal to. But Henry is a very suspicious man who does not trust people. This makes him hard to love as a good king is loved. What we need is another inspirational soldier like Henry V. Sadly Henry Tudor is not like that. He will work hard but I fear that rebellions may continue.

The end of my story

I hope the story of my family has been interesting – and I wonder what you have decided about what's it been like to live in the fifteenth century?

Activity

17 Why did the Earl of Warwick rebel against Edward IV?
18 Why did Richard III take the crown? Find at least two reasons.
19 Why did people rebel against Richard?
20 Most nobles stayed loyal to Henry VII despite some small rebellions. Why do you think they did not support those rebellions?
21 Anne said that many people think that nobles rushed into fighting wars because they were greedy for power. Do you agree that is why the nobles fought in the wars? Give two reasons for your answer (your answers to questions 17–19 will help you).

8

What can Anne Herbert tell us about life during the Wars of the Roses?

How do we know about Anne Herbert's life?

You might be wondering how we know so much about Anne Herbert. It's hard to find out very much about individuals in the fifteenth century apart from kings and queens and important nobles. However, we do know lots of basic information. All the details in the last few pages about Anne's husband, brother and sons are true. We know about them from government records. However, we don't know what they looked like or what kind of people they were – friendly, cheerful or bad-tempered.

What happened to Anne and her family?

Anne Herbert died in about 1486, aged about 53. She was buried alongside her husband, William, in Tintern Abbey. Her eldest son, William died not long afterwards. Her other son, Walter, worked for Henry VII although he was never highly rewarded. Anne's daughter Maud, who they had hoped would marry Henry Tudor (Henry VII), married the Earl of Northumberland instead.

What other evidence tells us about Anne and her life? It's a bit like putting together a jigsaw even though we don't have all the pieces. Here are the pieces we do have:

Activity

22 Which of the pieces of evidence about Anne do you think is the most interesting in the jigsaw below? Explain why you chose it.

23 Can you see a link between the ring (piece F) and the picture opposite (look at William's robes)? Explain what the link is.

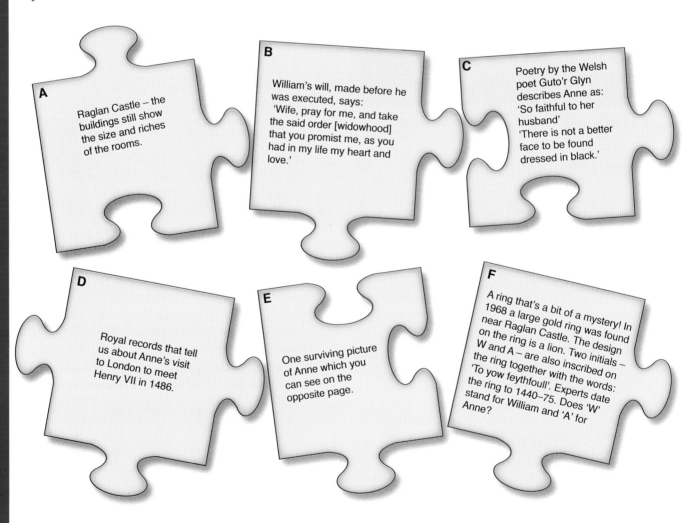

A Raglan Castle – the buildings still show the size and riches of the rooms.

B William's will, made before he was executed, says:
'Wife, pray for me, and take the said order [widowhood] that you promist me, as you had in my life my heart and love.'

C Poetry by the Welsh poet Guto'r Glyn describes Anne as:
'So faithful to her husband'
'There is not a better face to be found dressed in black.'

D Royal records that tell us about Anne's visit to London to meet Henry VII in 1486.

E One surviving picture of Anne which you can see on the opposite page.

F A ring that's a bit of a mystery! In 1968 a large gold ring was found near Raglan Castle. The design on the ring is a lion. Two initials – W and A – are also inscribed on the ring together with the words: 'To yow feythfoull'. Experts date the ring to 1440–75. Does 'W' stand for William and 'A' for Anne?

This picture shows William and Anne kneeling at the feet of a king. Anne's head-dress is typical of what women wore at the time. The men all have their hair cut short. Again this was the fashion, especially for men who had fought in the wars in France as William had. You can see William's badge of a lion on his robes.

The picture comes from a book that William and Anne had made for King Henry VI in either 1459 or 1460 to show their loyalty to Henry. Everything in it was written or drawn by hand so it was very expensive. We now know that the king in the picture is Henry VI. Historians used to think the king was Edward IV because William Herbert was one of Edward's closest supporters. However, Sonja Drimmer, a historian, spent a lot of time investigating the book and discovered that it had been made in 1459 or 1460 when Henry VI was still king and so it must be Henry in the picture. This shows that historians keep making new discoveries even about events 500 years ago.

Activity

24 How useful do you think the picture of Anne on this page is for historians?

25 Do you think it was a good idea to tell the story of the Wars of the Roses through Anne's imagined words? Explain why you did – or didn't – like this style of writing.

Summing up the Middle Ages

It's now time to sum up what you have learned about the Middle Ages. This section gives you some quick activities which look back over the Middle Ages. They aren't here to catch you out. They're here to help you show off how much you have learned!

A

B

C

D

E

F

G

H 1348

I

J MAGNA CARTA

K

L

M

N 1381

O

Activity

3 One way to tell the story of a period of history is to write a summary in just 100 words. Below are three examples. Your task is to sum up the Middle Ages in 100 words or less. You don't have to use full sentences because you can make your writing more memorable with repetition or even with a single word sentence. You could even write a poem. You can be as inventive as you like! Use the pictures opposite or the index of this book on page 132 to jog your thoughts. Good luck!

Prehistoric Britain

Hunters following herds for food. Archaeological finds at Starr Carr. Slowly, slowly, slowly hunters become farmers. Settling in one place. Centuries and centuries of farming begin. Archaeology at Skara Brae in Orkney. Avebury, Stonehenge and other stone circles. Who did they worship?

Discovering skills. Bronze, then iron tools and weapons. Hillforts like Danebury and Maiden Castle give shelter and defences. Trade with travellers from overseas. Tales of great soldiers called Romans. Julius Caesar came and went and came and went. Who's afraid of the Romans?

Roman Britain

More Romans, helped by Britons who want Roman riches. The legions march and conquer, march and conquer. Caratacus, Boudicca rebel and are defeated. Britain becomes Roman Britain. Forts, towns, roads, Latin, baths, aqueducts bringing water. Hadrian's Wall marks the edge of the empire.

Villas for the wealthy with heating, mosaics, slaves, all paid for by rich farming land. People of all races and nationalities arrive from all parts of the Empire – Africa, Palestine, Europe. One century passes, two, three, many, many lifetimes. Around 400AD the legions go home. What next? Who knows?

Anglo-Saxon England

Enter the Anglo-Saxons – raiders, soldiers, farmers, traders. Nobody knows how many, settling alongside the Britons. They're all farmers now – is the harvest good? Fear of hunger every year.

597AD Augustine brings Christianity, defence against the Devil. Bede at Jarrow, Cuthbert at Lindisfarne, the Lindisfarne Gospels, The Anglo-Saxon Chronicle, Beowulf, art that lasts for centuries. Then the Vikings – raiding, trading, raiding some more. Alfred of Wessex fights back. Alfred, Edward, Aethelflaed, Athelstan – names easily forgotten but names that made England one country, England united. What happened to the Anglo-Saxons? They're still here – our language, our place names, our shires, our Angle-land.

The Middle Ages – what was really important?

At the beginning of this book on pages 10–11 we introduced you to three groups of people – the fighters, the people who prayed and the people who worked. On these two pages we are going to sum up what happened to each group in the Middle Ages. We are going to decide whether their lives stayed much the same or changed a lot – and which changes were the most important.

Activity

You can see that there is a set of six cards for each group of people.

1 One card in each group has a mistake on it. Identify the card and decide what it should say.
2 Sort each set of cards into things that changed and things that stayed the same during the Middle Ages.
3 Which group of people saw the most continuity in their lives?
4 Which change in each set do you think was the most important? Explain your choice.

The fighters (the king and his nobles)

A
The king was still the most powerful and the richest person in the country.

B
The nobles wanted to be loyal to the king.

C
The king of England had conquered Wales and Scotland.

D
The nobles expected the king to rule fairly and ask them for advice. When King John did not do this they forced him to agree to **Magna Carta** in 1215, a set of rules about how to govern the country.

E
The nobles had **deposed** two kings (Edward II and Richard II) who had ruled unfairly and treated their nobles harshly.

F
Kings called Parliament when they needed taxes to pay for wars. The king also ended meetings of Parliament whenever he wished.

The people who worked (the common folk)

A
Most people still worked as farmers. Only about 10 per cent of people lived in towns.

B
Everyone still depended on the harvest for their food. If there was a poor harvest people went hungry.

C
People lived much shorter lives than most people do today. Forty was a good age, though some people did live much longer.

D
The **Black Death** led to the population doubling in size.

E
People still did not understand that germs cause diseases, so they could do little to prevent diseases killing people.

F
By 1500 everyone was free to live and work where they liked. Nobody was a **villein** any more, forced to work for their lord.

The people who prayed (the priests, monks and nuns)

A
Christianity was still the only religion in Britain.

B
The English Church was part of the Catholic Church whose head was the Pope in Rome.

C
On holy days and **saints'** days everyone had to work twice as hard as usual.

D
More pilgrims went to the tomb of Thomas Becket in Canterbury Cathedral than any other **pilgrimage** site in England.

E
Many churches had paintings of Heaven and Hell on their walls to warn people that they needed to live better lives.

F
There were hundreds of **monasteries** in England. The monks helped the poor and often taught children to read and write.

How can Dick Whittington help us sum up the Middle Ages?

Once upon a time there was a young man called Dick Whittington. Nowadays he's famous as the hero in a pantomime where he walks to London to make his fortune and ends up Lord Mayor of London. In fact, Dick Whittington was a real person. He grew up near Bristol, travelled to London to become a merchant, became very rich and between 1397 and 1419 he was chosen as Lord Mayor of London four times.

Whittington was also a very generous man. He spent a lot of money helping the people of London, and then in his will left £3 million at today's prices to pay for more projects to help Londoners. For example, he paid for:

- rebuilding of his parish church
- repair of St Bartholomew's Hospital and building a ward for unmarried mothers at St Thomas's Hospital
- building drinking fountains with clean water and public toilets seating 64 men and 64 women
- building two libraries
- building homes for elderly poor people.

The Whittington charity still helps the poor today.

Intelligent, thoughtful people

Dick Whittington's story tells us important things about the Middle Ages. We have spent time in this book on wars, rebellions and disease and it's easy to think of the Middle Ages as a horrible, terrible time when the people were always violent and selfish. However it's important to remember that people in the Middle Ages were just as clever and thoughtful as people today. Here are some examples that show the intelligence and thoughtfulness of medieval people:

- People did not rush to rebel and kill the king if he ruled unfairly. They tried to find ways of solving problems peacefully as they did when they created Magna Carta and called the first Parliaments.

- People worked hard to keep streets clean to avoid diseases spreading. Many people gave money to pay for fresh water supplies, public toilets and sewers to take away waste. People were fined for throwing rubbish in the streets.

- Ordinary people were interested in politics and national events. In 1381 and 1450 ordinary people marched to London to protest about bad government. They wanted to improve the way the king was ruling the country, not start a rebellion.

1381

Deeply religious people

Dick's story also tells us about the importance of religion. He spent his money helping people because he was generous but also because helping the poor meant he would spend less time in Purgatory and reach Heaven sooner after he died.

The most important thing to remember about life in Britain in the Middle Ages is that religion was central to almost everything that happened, as you can see on this diagram.

Everyone went to church at least once a week and believed in Heaven, Purgatory and Hell.

Vast amounts of money were spent celebrating religion by building cathedrals and churches.

People took great risks going on pilgrimages and on crusade.

There were many monasteries and convents where monks and nuns helped the poor and local people.

How did religion affect people's lives?

All holidays were 'holy days' and the plays people watched retold Bible stories.

Many people gave money to help the poor and local people because of their religious beliefs.

People believed that diseases were sent by God to punish them for not living as God wanted.

People believed that kings were chosen by God and they should not rebel against them.

Ordinary people were important too

It's easy to think that only kings and barons did important things in the Middle Ages. However there were many people like Dick Whittington all over England who helped the people around them. Take a look at these examples. Who do you think were more important – the kings or the ordinary people who did extraordinary things?

Whittington who spent vast amounts of money helping the people of London.

Edward I who united England and Wales by conquering Wales and started the first regular parliaments.

William Caxton who brought the first printing press to England. Printing helped many more people learn to read and helped spread knowledge and new ideas.

William the Conqueror who changed the royal family and killed thousands of people who rebelled against him.

The unknown people who built Durham cathedral and all the churches in the Middle Ages which still add great beauty to towns and villages.

Henry V who won the **Battle of Agincourt** against France and so made many people feel 'English' for the first time.

And finally …

So when you think about the Middle Ages, don't just think of wars, dirt, knights and disease. Think of generosity, religious beliefs, intelligence and the remarkable 'ordinary' people who built the world we live in today.

Glossary

Abbey The buildings where monks lived and prayed. The abbey church is the main building.

Abbot A title, meaning 'father', given to the head of a monastery.

Artillery Cannon or other large guns capable of firing over a large distance.

Battle of Agincourt A battle in 1415 in which the English, led by Henry V, beat the French.

Battle of Hastings A battle in 1066 in which William of Normandy beat King Harold of England.

Bayeux Tapestry A tapestry telling the story of the Norman Conquest, woven in England but designed by the Normans.

Bishop A leading churchman who was in charge of all the churches and monasteries in an area.

Black Death One of the most devastating epidemics of infectious disease resulting in the deaths of an estimated 75 to 200 million people and peaking in Europe in the years 1348–50.

Bubonic Plague An infectious disease which is believed to be the cause of the Black Death that swept through Europe in the fourteenth century. *See also* **Black Death**

Cavalry Soldiers who fought on horseback.

Chivalry Qualities that a knight was expected to have. This included bravery, courtesy and honour.

Christopher Columbus Italian explorer who reached the Americas in 1492 although he was really searching for China.

Civil war A war in which the people of one country fight each other.

Convent A building where nuns live.

Coronation The ceremony when a king or queen is crowned at the beginning of his or her reign.

Crossbow men Soldiers who used crossbows that fired bolts. They did not need as much training as an archer.

The Crusades A religious war between Christians and Muslims for control of the Holy Land.

Daoism A Chinese philosophy teaching that the natural world always tries to be in balance.

Depose Remove a king or queen from the throne.

Domesday Book A manuscript which records the Domesday Survey of much of England and parts of Wales completed in 1086.

Dukedom The lands belonging to a duke, a leading nobleman.

Excommunicate Forced to leave the Christian Church so unable to attend services or go to Heaven.

Hundred Years War A war between England and France that was fought intermittently between 1337 and the mid-1500s.

Illegitimate A child of parents who are not married to each other.

Inference Using clues to work out something the evidence does not tell you directly.

Interdict Punishment from the Catholic Church that prevented people from taking part in baptisms, marriages and burials.

King Arthur The legendary king of Britain who fought against invading Saxons after the Roman armies left Britain. There is no evidence of Arthur being a real person.

Longbow A tall bow – usually as long as the person who fires it. Medieval longbows could fire arrows over 300 metres and possibly pierce armour.

Magna Carta Agreement in 1215 between King John and his barons about how the king should rule the country.

Masons Highly-skilled craftsmen who carved and shaped stone to build cathedrals and other buildings. The master mason was the man in charge of the building and played a big part in designing it.

Mercenaries Soldiers who fought for money rather than loyalty or service to their king.

Merchant A trader who makes his money by buying and selling goods such as wool or food.

Monasteries Buildings where monks live.

Normandy A region of France that had its own independent ruler, the Duke.

Normans The people of Normandy.

Pilgrimage A journey made with the aim of visiting a holy site, such as the city of Jerusalem.

Poll tax The poll or 'head' tax was payable by every person in England. The 1381 poll tax was a cause of the Peasants' Revolt.

Refugee Someone who runs away from a disaster, war or poverty.

Saint A person (usually dead) whom the Catholic Church has decided has achieved a remarkable level of holiness.

Saint Cuthbert An important saint in the medieval Catholic Church. After his death he became one of the most important saints in the North of England – he is buried in Durham Cathedral.

Saxon The people who, along with the Angles, came to Britain after the Roman period.

Sedan chair An example of a wheelless vehicle. A chair placed inside a box is carried by two or four bearers who lift the poles attached to the box.

Sin of gluttony One of the seven deadly sins of the medieval Church, characterised by overeating.

Sin of greed One of the seven deadly sins of the medieval Church, characterised by a desire to gather wealth and riches.

Sin of sloth One of the seven deadly sins of the medieval Church, characterised by extreme laziness.

Souls The spirit of a person that many religions think either lives on after death or goes to Heaven.

Standard A king or lord's personal flag.

The Tower The Tower of London, the castle built by William the Conqueror.

Vaccination Medicine designed to give a person immunity from a disease.

Viking The people from Scandinavia who came to Britain as invaders and traders from the 8th to the 11th centuries.

Villein A villager who was not free and had to work on the lord's land for a number of days every week without pay.

Wars of the Roses A civil war fought intermittently in England between 1455 and 1487.

World Heritage Site A place (such as a forest, mountain, lake, island, desert, monument, building, complex, or city) that is listed by the United Nations as of special cultural or physical significance.

Index